AC

MW01227447

"I bootstrapped and sold my first startup, and James's principles are valuable for any company no matter the size."

—Guy Diedrich, SVP and Global Innovation Officer, Cisco Systems

"James knows firsthand that bootstrapping doesn't just apply to startups—some of the oldest industries, like insurance, have only been disrupted from within by bootstrapped efforts of corporate innovators. This book is for those visionaries, too."

—Rob Galbraith, Founder and CEO, Forestview Insights, and author of *The End of Insurance As We Know It*

"The reality is that we all exit our business one day. James Benham is a compelling thought leader on how bootstrapping can maximize the value you exit with. Whether you're one or twenty years away from an exit, Be Your Own VC offers bootstrapping principles that every innovator can apply."

—Simon Bedard, Founder & CEO, Exit Advisory Group

"Benham nails it, as expected. Sometimes your best investor is yourself. Nobody understands cash flow management and bootstrapping as well as James, and the book is jam-packed with insights and war stories for the growing entrepreneur."

—Andrew J. Sherman, Partner, Seyfarth Shaw, and author of 26 books on business growth and capital formation

"As construction is the world's oldest industry, James and I have had to work hard to pull it into the future through technology. His experience has inspired me and many others to bootstrap their vision, think like a startup, and find the right partners to have an impact."

—Ricardo Khan, Senior Vice President and Chief Innovation Officer, STO Building Group

JAMES M. BENHAM

BE
YOUR OWN
VC

10 BOOTSTRAPPING PRINCIPLES TO GENERATE CASH AND KEEP CONTROL

HOUNDSTOOTH
PRESS

Copyright © 2022 James M. Benham
All rights reserved.

Be Your Own VC
10 Bootstrapping Principles to Generate Cash and Keep Control

ISBN 978-1-5445-3569-2 Hardcover
978-1-5445-3567-8 Paperback
978-1-5445-3568-5 Ebook
978-1-5445-3805-1 Audiobook

Liz Beechinor, Editor

CONTENTS

To my family—
for always being there with support,
encouragement, and love.

INTRODUCTION

D epending on the hour of the day, I'm an entrepreneur, I'm an investor, or I'm a corporate innovator. I started a business in 2001 that I'm still running. I sold a product company, and I invest the proceeds in things I care about. I advise companies on how innovative technology can write their next chapter.

I've learned that all of these roles require a bootstrapping mindset. I'd argue that most professional roles do. Unfortunately, that mindset isn't taught enough. We glorify stories of startups fundraising and scaling at breakneck speed over the stories of steady growth and hard-fought profit. We champion stories of overnight inventions in research and development (R&D) labs over stories of what it took to get executive buy-in. We boil down success stories to the pithiest 280 characters that will draw attention on social media, but what we really need is the full, grueling story to learn from.

Consider that five hundred thousand new businesses are started every year in the U.S., and less than 5 percent of those will receive outside funding. Five percent. If you're on social media or have attended any events in the tech or startup world, that percentage may shock you because it seems like everyone is pursuing and getting funding. That's not the case. Ninety-five percent of businesses will have to bootstrap to survive. Those 5 percent that do get funding will have to learn to bootstrap to pay back their investors and avoid needing more funding.

At the end of an innovator's journey, the value they walk away with is tied directly to their track record of bootstrapping. In a world with more access to capital, debt, and crowdsourcing than ever before, I don't see bootstrapping taught enough—not in MBA classes, startup accelerators, innovation conferences, or the entrepreneurial publications we all read.

This book is my effort to share the full story of a bootstrapped entrepreneur in order to communicate the value (and multi-million-dollar results) of a bootstrapping mindset. Figuratively, I often say a bootstrapped entrepreneur is someone willing to build what they have to so they can then build what they love. Technically, a bootstrapper is an entrepreneur who takes a small number of resources, generates a profit, and reinvests that profit in growth. A bootstrapper does this over and over as they scale to avoid taking on outside investment.

Typically, bootstrapping is a longer road than securing debt or funding up front, but it fortifies an organization that is sustainable, profitable, and built on survival. I've learned that bootstrapping a business creates a certain culture among the people involved. When you encounter a group of people who have had to focus on breaking even or making a profit every year without the safety net of outside funds, they behave differently. They act differently. They think differently.

Whether you're an entrepreneur, investing in an entrepreneur, or an intrapreneur trying to disrupt corporate bureaucracy, I wrote this book for you. I've seen the bootstrapping mindset transform the lives and businesses of all three groups. This book is a compilation of bootstrapping principles I've followed in my own business for more than twenty years. I've never found absolute advice to be very useful—"Do exactly this" or "Don't do this"—just because you're reading my book doesn't mean I know your business, background, or vision. Therefore, this is a guidebook—not an instruction manual. Just like any good travel guide, it's a summary of my first-hand experience, but I'm not planning your trip—that's your job. I believe bootstrapping principles can get you to any destination.

At the beginning of every new business, investment, or innovation project, the questions are the same: *how do we get started, and then how do we keep it going?* The entrepreneur or intrapreneur usually has a clear, and personal, connection to the challenge they want to solve.

They have an idea of where their customers will come from. They have a vision of their office, team, and lifestyle as the effort scales. In addition to their personal and professional experience, there is no shortage of resources and voices offering advice. From marketing hacks to suggestions on how to raise capital to "That definitely won't work," everyone seems to know the best and only way forward. Your own intuition can easily get quieter as the free advice gets louder.

Leading a business is an incredibly exciting prospect. It's also scary, stressful, lonely, and fraught with risk. It's easy to start your journey by thinking, *I have to find somebody who can convince somebody else of why I should start this business. I need a venture capitalist (VC) or corporate partner or someone smarter than me.* What I encourage you to keep in mind is that *you* have the vision, and there's a way for you to build your dream and be your own VC. There's a way for you to invest in your own team, generate your own cash, and create your own culture. There's a way that I was taught and that I've sharpened in practice. My way can be much harder, but it can deliver unimaginable value.

This book will not bash VCs, private equity firms, or angel investors—in fact, it's written with them in mind. (I've even invested in some venture funds myself.) They have just as much to gain from supporting a bootstrapping mindset in their founders. The bootstrapping mindset doesn't prohibit outside capital or even assume you're an entrepreneur at all. It simply means you're willing to build what you have to so you can build what you want to. It means you establish a series of questions, values, and systems that help you fund your idea with the right partners and maximize your equity.

Bootstrapping is about self-sustainability, resourcefulness, and survival above all. When times are good, you fund your own growth and enjoy the upside. When times get tough, you are better equipped to live within your means, manage your costs, and outlast competitors. Without mastering bootstrapping, I've seen too many friends get fired from their own companies, lose money on careless investments, and get shut down on efforts they had hoped would bring their company into the future.

My team at JBKnowledge has embraced bootstrapping over the last twenty years to build, operate, and sell technology companies. From a $5,000 investment from my dad to a successful exit and millions in profit, we've learned a few things about working within our means and maintaining our ownership.

As I'm writing this in 2022, it would be tone deaf not to acknowledge that bootstrapping implies you have the privilege of starting with boots and a safety net—in the form of savings, family investment, or even just a free place to live. The reality is that many people start a business without bootstraps or even a pair of boots. I worked really hard for what I built, but the fact remains I started with a small but critical investment and loan from my dad and the priceless mentorship he's provided throughout my life. For many entrepreneurs, that's not a given. Many entrepreneurs have a vision, but they didn't grow up with serial entrepreneurs in their family, and they didn't start learning these lessons as soon as they could talk. To imply that all entrepreneurs can just pull themselves up by their bootstraps is unfair—that's not the starting point for many. The starting point may be locating bootstraps. Through my work as an adjunct professor at Texas A&M University and a Regent at Texas Southern University, I've learned that education is one of the most important producers of bootstraps, and we all have a responsibility to bolster that pipeline of talent and share access where it hasn't been available before.

When I joined the Board of Regents at Texas Southern, I thought I'd be leading entrepreneurial discussions and startup workshops, but my focus has instead settled on a program for young pilots. That's right, teaching college students to fly planes. Flying is a hobby I waited to pursue until I'd "made it" only to realize it may have helped me "make it" much sooner. The perspective I have from the cockpit echoes so much of the internal dialogue I experienced as a bootstrapped entrepreneur that I thought, *These students should start here.* And man, wings are the new bootstraps.

The ultimate reward of both flying and bootstrapping is freedom. Freedom to navigate your own path and pursue the horizons only you can see—uninhibited by paved roads and other drivers who may not have interests aligned with your own. I hope this book helps you maximize that freedom.

My story is told chronologically, with a few flashbacks and flashforwards when necessary. In each chapter, I've singled out the bootstrapping principle that solidified into a mantra for me during that time period. I hope you find inspiration in repeating these principles to yourself on the hard days. (You can also find the full list at the end of the book.) I've written my experiences as I remember them, and I hope my writing does justice to everyone who impacted me along the way. If you walk away from this book feeling inspired and capable of pursuing your dream business—with or without outside investment—I hope you'll reach out and let me know how I can help.

CHAPTER 1

CASH:
THE FUEL FOR
THE BUSINESS

B ecoming an entrepreneur definitely was not an accident
for me. My father started several businesses. My grandfather ran his own farm. My great-grandfather ran his
own medical practice. My great-great-grandfather owned and
ran a sanatorium. I'm a fifth-generation entrepreneur, and
very few people in my family have worked as employees for
anybody else. Aunts, uncles, cousins, parents, grandparents,

and so on led organizations they started, scaled, and sold, and then, they started again. Because of this, I've always had the utmost respect for accidental entrepreneurs who had no direct examples or mentors in their families like I did. If this is you, I'm incredibly humbled you're reading this, and I'm excited to share the family education.

My father was the ultimate example of an entrepreneur. My upbringing was a continuous lesson on being your own boss and best employee. It was my father, not my educators, who taught me the fundamentals of starting a company, leading a team, and operating a sustainable business. My father wasn't a "founder" in today's use of the word. I wouldn't even describe him as a disruptor. He was something much less appreciated but much more valuable—a builder and an operator.

My dad taught me that regardless of how you intend to *start* a business—whether through invention, innovation, or process improvement—you cannot *grow* a business without consistent, persistent hard work. It's important you accept this truth from day one. I continue to meet entrepreneurs, bootstrapped and not, who believe if they work hard enough for twelve months, they can coast forever after. It's easy to think, *When I get to $1 million in revenue, I'll hire people to do the leg work. I'll show up to the office when I want, be The Big Boss, make the big decisions, and leave at four to play some golf.*

There are lines of work where this is plausible—entrepreneurism is not one of them. I've seen five generations of proof. After twenty years, multiple profitable companies, and a major exit, I don't work weekends as much and can afford to vacation and delegate, but the responsibility I carry has grown, and the accountability has only become heavier.

My dad always says, "Don't be a lazy farmer." It means that no matter how successful your harvest and how much wealth or fame it brings, there's no substitute for hard work when the next planting season comes. Get up early, work hard, and go to bed tired. History continues to prove that most of the time, successful people simply outwork their competition. My dad is a prime example of that.

Another saying my dad may as well have tattooed on my forehead is "Cash is king." From watching my father start and grow multiple businesses and running my own, I've learned that nothing beats cash on hand—in good years but especially in bad. It takes discipline, sacrifice, and a lot of productive paranoia to have cash in the bank at all times, but that's exactly what you owe yourself, your vision, and your team. In order to get there, you may have to double your expense projections and halve your revenue expectations, sacrifice your own compensation, and prioritize paying off debt as quickly as possible. Simple, right?

Not really, but it's worth it. My dad was the first to show me how it's done.

Cash is king.

Nothing beats cash on hand, especially in an economic disruption. To build a sustainable business, seek opportunities to generate recurring cash with low overhead.

My Dad: The Farmer, Sailor, and Teflon Salesman

In 1943 rural Mississippi, a five-year-old and his dad were prepping a tractor for planting season. The dad dismounted the tractor to hook up a piece of equipment to the back. When he was done, the five-year-old confidently hopped into the driver's seat of the tractor for the first time ever and drove it out of the barn. What did the dad say?

"Nothing. That was a good thing about my father. He let me run. I'm sure he was terrified, but he would let me do it regardless."

That five-year-old was my father, Jim Benham, and his dad was my grandfather, Harvey Benham. By the age of eight, my dad had plowed his first field solo, and by the age of nine, he had driven a log truck full of oak and pine trees to the mill.

When my dad was three years old, his family left New Orleans to purchase and run a corn, oat, and soybean farm in southern Mississippi. My grandfather had been a city employee in New Orleans and claimed they had to leave after he'd "voted wrong"—meaning he had not voted for the new governor (when the new governor was elected, there were rumors that any city employee who hadn't voted for him had their ballot marked and was shown the door). My grandfather had an agricultural degree from Purdue and always kept a meticulously curated greenhouse. After college, he had even lived in Liberia, Africa, working on rubber-tree farms for Firestone Tires. So when the time came to leave New Orleans, he decided to become a farmer.

My grandfather was a gregarious, charismatic man, so it's no surprise he made the leap from loving plants to confidently buying a farm. He trusted in his ability to figure things out and charm people into supporting him. And he did figure things out, though he would never go down in the hall of fame of farmers. Any sense of urgency my grandfather had in his DNA had been neatly packaged and passed down to his son, Jim. While my grandfather ran the farm successfully, he never worked harder than break even. If he got ahead, he enjoyed time off, and he took long lunch breaks; meanwhile, his son went out to work the fields during those breaks, unable to feel anything less than urgency. They butted heads often due to this difference in personality—but they were probably good for each other because of it. My dad inherited his mother's German work ethic and seriousness; my grandfather kept him from turning too many waking hours into working hours.

The farm helped my dad learn a valuable work ethic and develop a love for anything with a motor. By eighteen, he was ready for adventure, so he decided to join the navy. He credits this decision to a memory from when he was eight years old, standing in a field on the farm while a V-Tail Bonanza plane flew overhead (the farm was on an early visual-flying route). He watched it irreverently cut through the clouds and said aloud, "I'm going to do that." So he joined the navy, intent on becoming a pilot.

When my dad arrived in San Diego, he volunteered to take the naval pilot-training entry exam. Unfortunately, he didn't score high enough to get into flight school. He was disappointed, but my dad loves to "work the problem," as he always says. He decided to find his own route to becoming a pilot while the navy trained him to be a Fire Control Technician.

As a Fire Control Technician, my dad learned to aim naval destroyer-ship guns at targets in air, on land, and at sea. After basic training in California and Nevada, he learned his specific trade at a naval school in Illinois. Two important things came from this training: a loathing of Midwest winters, and his first flying lessons, funded by his beloved Uncle Tom Benham, at a private, grass airfield. My dad still has the logbooks from those training flights and can narrate through each and every page.

In 1957, my dad was assigned to the USS *Mansfield*, where he'd live until 1960. His stories of his time on ship align with most movies from that era—the comradery of those stuck in small quarters, an optimism for the open ocean, and an awe for the power of the U.S. military. In fact, my dad is the only person I know who has seen atomic bombs many times the size of those dropped on Hiroshima explode and lived to tell about it.

The USS *Mansfield* traveled all over the Pacific Ocean, but its primary mission was as an observation ship for nuclear-bomb tests. My dad personally watched over twenty nuclear bombs explode in the Pacific. Standing on deck nearly twenty miles away from the impact, he would watch the shock waves form a column of water that shot straight up into the air, with red, yellow, and purple serpents of smoke racing to the top until a mushroom cloud formed. Within twenty minutes, that cloud would be directly overhead of him standing on the *Mansfield* deck. It's crazy to think how testing like this would cause a world crisis today, and my dad might as well have been watching it with a bag of overpriced popcorn.

My dad was in the navy four years, and during the latter two, he saved up all of his leave (vacation days), applied to Louisiana State University (LSU), got in, and was able to pay for his first year with the cash the navy traded him for his unused leave. Dad always found the cash to fund his next idea—and he always had a next idea.

Dad started at LSU in 1960. While taking ten hours of electrical engineering coursework a semester, he worked full time in the physics department, running a particle accelerator. In addition, he worked two part-time jobs: one at a filling station, and one at a hospital, repairing electrical equipment on call. Dad knew that cash flow and savings gave him options when he needed them.

During his sophomore year, some girls from his church set my dad up on a blind date with their sorority sister Mary. They spent an entire LSU versus Ole Miss football game talking. My dad jokes that he wasn't sure if Mary liked him or his blue Jaguar more. Regardless, she married him nine months later. Mom was nineteen; Dad was twenty-four, and after marrying, they moved in together to finish college.

By 1965, Dad had his undergrad degree and had started his MBA coursework and his first company. My dad's brother-in-law Andy was studying to be an ear, nose, and throat (ENT) doctor at Tulane University. He told my dad about a device his professor had invented. While the professor had built the plans for the device, he had no intentions of producing or distributing it—so my dad decided to do that himself.

My mom remembers my dad on the kitchen floor, building his first prototype of a portable nystagmography device—a diagnostic tool that helped doctors measure eye movements and irregularities. The tool was a physical user interface that could be placed over digital recording devices to help doctors read and analyze the results. After forming Medical Systems Limited, Dad borrowed $600 from a friend, built and sold his first nystagmography device, and found a local manufacturer to produce parts to build the devices in bulk. The business only ran for three or four years, with Andy helping sell to his ENT doctor contacts and Dad managing the books and production. The per-unit margins weren't high enough to grow a big business, but they made enough to cover their costs plus a little.

While my dad was working full time, taking classes, and operating Medical Systems Limited in 1970, he received a phone call from the hospital where he had worked during his undergrad years. A friend at the hospital let him know that they were planning to contract out all of their electrical equipment maintenance, and she wanted my dad to pursue the contract because she liked working with him. Dad entertained the idea and scheduled a meeting at the hospital. At the end of a successful meeting, they asked my dad, "What's the name of your business?" and Dad made up "Hospital Equipment Service Company (HESCO)" on the spot and later registered it.

HESCO turned out to be a cash cow, and Dad was the only employee. He secured recurring monthly maintenance contracts with multiple hospital networks, rarely had to work more than forty hours a week, and had almost no overhead. He was making over $100,000 a year in the 1970s, equivalent to over half a million dollars a year today. This allowed him to quit his full-time job and focus on being an entrepreneur.

He eventually shut down Medical Systems Limited due to growing regulatory requirements for medical devices, but he kept HESCO Machine Shop, another company he'd registered to build the parts for the ENT diagnostic device. The machine shop was operating at break even with roughly five employees, but it was a real estate property full of equipment assets that Dad knew he could sell for cash or use in future businesses.

The 1970s taught my dad the lesson that was basically branded onto me as his son: cash is king. Especially recurring, low-overhead cash like the kind my dad was making through HESCO. He was learning that you want to have a business that sells to grow, not to survive.

In 1979, Dad finally sold the machine shop in what was essentially an asset sale. At this point, only his HESCO business remained. Then, he received a call from a man named Julius Beard. Julius had recently helped start a Teflon business with four brothers. Unfortunately, they had pushed him out, but he was still motivated to build a Teflon enterprise. Julius pitched my dad on the opportunities to sell Teflon services to multiple industries and his expertise in manufacturing it. Most importantly, Dad really liked the guy. To this day, Dad talks about Julius like the brother he never had. "Even Julius' wife used to say that God put us together, and she didn't even believe in God," Dad told me once.

With a $150,000 loan and the cash flow from HESCO, Dad and Julius started Industrial Plastics & Machine (IPM). Dad insisted that Julius take 50 percent of the company. Julius countered that 50 percent was not warranted since he wasn't bringing any cash to the table. But Dad wanted Julius invested and committed, and Dad knew *nothing* about Teflon.

He wanted Julius to stick around and have as much incentive as himself to make the business a success, so Julius agreed to own 50 percent of the company with the condition that my father was the president.

However, within a year of starting IPM, they were running out of capital, and their wives had nicknamed them "Gloom and Doom" due to their pre-apocalyptic moods. Originally, IPM was intended to service chemical plants manufacturing Teflon, but after twelve months, they realized that to survive and grow, they'd have to go into manufacturing Teflon themselves.

But manufacturing is a capital-intensive process, so they needed clients to fund it. My dad understood that oil-manufacturing plants used a lot of Teflon, so he went to the Lafayette, Louisiana, industrial district, where oil businesses lined the street. He went door to door, not making a single sale. He did, however, meet one company executive who told him, "We don't need your product, but call these guys and tell them I sent you." He called everyone on that list, and every single one of them chose to switch their Teflon orders to IPM. He had a 100 percent hit rate on that list because it came with a personal referral from someone who had met Dad for the twenty minutes after he stepped into his office. With these new clients, they were off the brink of shutting down, IPM became cash-flow positive, and the manufacturing business was up and running.

Now, they needed more clients to grow, so my dad turned to the Yellow Pages (there was no internet in 1980) and visited the LSU Library section of phone books from across the country. He spent three days combing through the phone book of every major city and making a handwritten list of every company in the "Plastic" section. By cold calling these businesses, they tripled their client list in three months. My dad was the first person to tell me, "Most of sales is just asking for the business. I'd call and say, 'My name is Jim Benham with IPM in Baton Rouge. We mold Teflon, and I'm looking for business. Do you have any need for Teflon parts? If yes, do you have a job I can quote for you right now?' Everyone was curious for a quote."

What I later learned is that the quotes were also a big part of their success. You see, my dad had been following the growth of UPS, and he realized he could use it to get Teflon parts shipped countrywide in as little as two days. All of IPM's competitors operated on a two- to three-week shipping schedule for the same cost. While competitors eventually caught on to the efficiency of UPS shipping, they were too late; Dad and Julius had already swiped many of their clients. By the early 2000s, IPM was bringing in $10 million a year with thirty-five employees and an expansive manufacturing facility.

In 2004, Julius was ready to sell. While my dad wasn't, he loved and respected Julius too much to deny him retirement. They sold IPM for exactly the price they desired to an Italian company that made the mistake of admitting how badly they wanted to buy it. My dad had no incentive to sell, the company was doing brilliantly, so the buyers had no negotiating room. It was a good place to negotiate from, and they sealed the deal.

My dad's entrepreneurial journey was a lot like him: logical, quietly diligent, and accomplished without ceremony. Personality-wise, we are very different. I have the charisma and boisterous nature of his father and the social propensities of my mother. I love hyperbole and getting people *really* amped about things I get amped about. My dad is an introvert and loves accuracy and subtlety. When I was confirming some of these names and dates with him, he would get stuck wanting to get every detail correct. If he couldn't remember, he'd decisively say, "I don't know, let's move on," implying that I should leave that part out since we were unsure.

My dad and I are also very similar. We work until the job is done and then keep working until the next job becomes obvious. We are not timid about our objectives and have never shied away from selling. We know what we want out of life, and loudly or quietly, we'll figure out how to get it. Thanks to these similarities, my dad would eventually invest in me as a business partner, like he did Julius. For all his focus on numbers, feasibility, and cash, Dad taught me to value the person behind the business above all else.

CHAPTER 2

DEBT
SUCKS

Two big factors in generating and maintaining cash flow are minimizing expenses and minimizing debt, both of which consume cash. While my dad consistently taught me to avoid debt while growing up, when I arrived at business school, I was surprised how many educators pushed using leverage. They often taught about using debt to finance a business activity. While it may sound wonderful conceptually, leverage bites hard both ways. It can help you take a small amount of cash and buy something much more expensive (think about all those late-night real estate commercials that promote buying and flipping homes for no money down). But when times get even a little tough, debt payments can bite so hard they eat all your food. There are many, many examples of this that business leaders like to forget because they're so painful. Just look at the dot-com collapse of 2000 or the Great Recession that started in 2008 as stark examples of how badly debt can sink businesses and individuals when a downturn occurs. Those monthly payments are unavoidable and end up consuming your free cash flow at a time when revenue is also declining. Thanks to interest, the cost of the goods you buy with debt also becomes much more expensive. Just look at housing: a thirty-year fixed-rate mortgage can *double* the cost of a house over time. If you save up for what you need, use debt cautiously, and pay cash as much as possible, you're setting yourself up for a much better night's sleep.

There are some incredible courses out there on managing and minimizing debt. One I recommend to everyone is Financial Peace University by Dave Ramsey. Minimizing debt is a principle I first learned from my dad that was later reinforced by Dave Ramsey and has influenced every financial decision in bootstrapping my businesses since. It's an easy concept that is hard to embrace in our current climate of credit cards and low-interest loans. It doesn't mean avoiding debt entirely, but it does mean getting out from under it quickly.

Bootstrapping a business, or even a new effort at an existing business, may require capital you don't have. Debt can be your best friend when you don't want to give up ownership, but it can be your worst enemy when your business doesn't perform as planned.

PRINCIPLE:

Get out, and stay out, of debt.

Use debt as little as possible and pay it off as fast as possible. When revenue declines, debt has no sympathy and can't be cut as quickly as expenses.

Saturdays at the Teflon Factory

Every Saturday growing up, my dad took me to his Teflon manufacturing plant. The first thing we did when we arrived was check the mail and separate out all the checks the company had received. Dad would total them up and prep them for deposit on our way home. While he was opening the envelopes, Dad would remind me why we were there and why this mattered.

"You have to keep an eye on your money. No one will care about it as much as you. If you're not checking your accounts and verifying the cash coming in and going out, it's easy to lose sight of what you're making and spending. That's how you get yourself in trouble, and once you're in trouble, you have to make hard decisions, like letting people go or borrowing more money. You can trust others to help with your accounting, but you better be double checking the numbers."

So every Saturday, we deposited the checks ourselves.

After opening the mail, we'd grab push brooms and sweep as much of the nearly eighty thousand square feet of warehouse space as we could. I remember thinking, *This guy has dozens of employees, why are we cleaning the floors?* I finally mustered the nerve to ask one Saturday, and he replied, "This is how I get eyes on what's happening in my business. I manage by walking around. I see which machinery looks like it needs maintenance or who has too many files piled on their desk. It also reminds me and everyone else that if push comes to shove, I'll sweep the floors if that's what it takes to keep this business sustainable."

On those Saturdays, I learned a lot about what Dad's

business did and how it made money. I never worked as an employee at his business; he wouldn't hire me, but I walked next to him every week for years to see what was going on in the business. I began to understand the product, how it was made, what it sold for, and who it was sold to.

I later understood that Dad was also showing his team that he was accessible for an entire day a week. I've learned that many employees find it hard to be open and candid with company leaders—especially if those employees don't report to you directly. Most of your employees, no matter their roles, have a reserved list in their heads just for the top leader. Passively saying "My door's always open" or "Contact me any time" is admirable but not very actionable. Employees will always reserve the serious or creative stuff on that list in their heads until they see you in person and are feeling brave. Most employees will wait until the day you walk by and ask them directly, "What are you working on? Anything I can help with, or anything we can be doing better?" You can build trust, communication, and accessibility simply by being present in both chaotic and calm times—or simply by sweeping the floors and asking them directly to share their thoughts.

Not only did I learn about his business on these Saturdays, but I also learned about my dad. If your kid doesn't understand your passion, they won't be as forgiving when you have to work late or miss a recital. Especially as a bootstrapper, you're going to be hustling more than a lot of other parents, so make sure your kids understand what you do and why you do it. I've taken my kids to many of my speaking events; they know my office well, and I even take them on client visits occasionally.

Whatever I can do to demonstrate to them what I do all day and where their food comes from helps them appreciate my business and the time I spend on it so much more.

Each Saturday before we left the Teflon plant, Dad would check one more number: the UPS shipping bill for that week. While this bill was an important expense for the company, it was also a key indicator of the amount of product that had been shipped out and how much revenue had been made that week. Dad would tell me that having three to five simple numbers that tell you how your business is doing is critical. His top two numbers were the weekly checks received and UPS shipping bill.

Tracking critical numbers, managing by walking around, and sweeping the floors, my dad taught me that all three of these would help identify opportunities and problems in the business long before they happened and avoid drastic measures (and debt) to remedy problems discovered too late.

My First Bootstrapped Business

At twelve years old, I realized I needed my own money and my own way of making it. It all started because my mom, an avid antique collector, took me with her around south Louisiana to antique stores. I surprised my mom, and myself, with how hard I fell for antiques. There was something about the history and the value maintained in that history. I also loved that the pieces had already made it a century or two and would likely last many more. I decided I wanted an antique writing desk and found one that was over 150 years old. So, I needed to start making money to buy it.

I asked my dad if I could work for him at his company,

and he replied, "Son, I'm not going to let you work for me. You need to figure things out on your own. Go get a job, or start your own business."

I spent some time thinking about a viable business for a twelve-year-old, and it finally came to me: I could cut grass! I went back to Dad.

"Hey, Dad, can I use the lawnmower to start a lawn business? I want to cut people's grass."

"Nope," he said in the very direct manner my dad says everything.

"What do you mean?" I said, only mildly surprised.

"No. It's my lawnmower."

"Okay, how do I get a lawnmower so I can cut grass?" I asked, giving in to curiosity over frustration.

"I'll give you a loan with no interest, but you have to pay me back all the money you borrow before you can start keeping any money from your business." I accepted eagerly and decided to do the math later.

My father lent me the money, and we bought a lawnmower. When we got home, he recorded the purchase in a logbook and wrote down the loan amount; I signed it, then he countersigned. You'd think he wasn't sure I was going to pay him back! But he was teaching me that every business requires capital or assets, and if you go into debt to get them, you have to pay it off quickly so you can start making money. Any money you make while you have debt, he explained, isn't exclusively yours.

I secured my first few neighborhood customers and built a good client base, which allowed me to pay off the lawnmower quickly. After I paid off the lawnmower, I saved up money, bought an edger, and started charging more to edge. Then I saved up money and bought a blower so I could easily blow the grass off sidewalks. Somewhere in there, I also bought that 150-year-old antique writing desk.

Looking back, it was remarkably simple. I borrowed a tiny amount of money to buy the first piece of equipment I needed. Then I used the profit from that operation—*after* I paid off the debt—to buy the next piece of equipment. I was able to charge more by offering additional services, made more profit, and bought the next piece of equipment. Eventually, I didn't need more equipment, and I'd paid off all my debt and generated positive cash flow. It was an amazingly simple lesson that permeated the rest of my business career. Fast forward to 2007, our first good year at JBKnowledge, paying off our debt would be key to surviving 2008 through 2010.

CHAPTER 3

BUILD WHAT YOU HAVE TO

The first software application I ever developed was for my lawn-mowing business. My clients weren't paying me within a reasonable amount of time, so I programmed an application that would generate and print an official-looking invoice, then I'd place the paper invoice on their doorstep or the windshield of their car. I'll never forget one not-so-amused client who called me exclaiming, "What twelve-year-old knows how to generate an invoice!" I told him I wouldn't have had to learn if he'd paid his bill on time.

I didn't start my lawn-mowing business because I dreamt of building a landscaping empire. I had allergies, my clients paid late, and Louisiana summers are sweltering. I just needed the money. When you think about starting your first "grownup" business, it's easy to get into the mindset of "I will build my dream business, and I won't compromise on my vision. I won't build anything I don't love." If you're bootstrapping your effort, this is a luxury you can't afford.

Every innovator I meet has a very clear vision of what they want to start building. They have experienced a problem personally, watched someone else fail to fix a problem, or have a solution to a problem they see coming in the future.

Unfortunately, a real problem plus a brilliant solution doesn't always equal a successful business. You need product-market fit, marketing and sales, a pricing strategy, customer service, human resources, and a slew of other functions that cost money before a business can make money. So many brilliant business ideas never get off the ground for two big reasons:

1. They fail to pivot their solution to what the market needs and will pay for right now.

2. They spend too much time and money building their offering before proving it through sales.

This is why I say a bootstrapping mindset starts with being willing to build what you have to in order to build what you want to. This might mean building less sexy service or product offerings and sacrificing the ideal for the practical. It also might mean generating cash from what you know will sell to invest the profit in what you want to sell.

Build what you have to so you can build what you want to.

It will take time to build your dream business if you want to maintain control of it. Figure out what you have to build to earn revenue and cover expenses now so that you can generate profit to build your vision later.

Science Fair-Winning Software

When I was eleven, my dad ran for city council and needed a computer to manage his campaign. Once he was elected, he let me have the 486 Gateway 2000 computer in a rare moment of ignoring his debt principles. MS-DOS batch files never looked as sexy as they did in 1991. I still remember the cow-print box, the volume of every click of that keyboard, and battling the lint that would obstruct the mouse's ball. I was hooked, and I didn't even have the internet yet. I taught myself how to build programs, write software, and run an operating system on that beauty.

My mom was always convinced I was playing games or looking at porn on that computer, but I wasn't; I was falling in love with the technology. She'd catch me on the computer late at night and say, "Stop playing games," to which I'd reply, indignantly, "Mom, I wrote a software program." She didn't believe me, or even understand what I meant, until four years later.

I was fifteen when my tenth grade teacher said, "You all have to do a science-fair project." I went to an engineering-focused STEM school, and you weren't uncool if you competed in the science fair; you were uncool if you didn't. But I didn't want to be too nerdy, so I thought I'd do one of those volcano experiments. You know, where you make a volcano sculpture erupt? Earth-shattering idea. I was a red-blooded, American male, I told myself, and I could do something destructively macho at the nerd fair.

But at the end of the day, it didn't feel right. I'd learned this software thing on my new Gateway computer, and I knew that'd be more impressive to the other nerds. I realized that if I wanted to compete and be competitive, I had to build what was necessary, not just what I wanted. At the time, I was really fascinated by the German Enigma code cracked by mathematicians during World War II—I had seen several documentaries on it. Google didn't exist yet, so I went to the library and checked out books on encryption after watching those documentaries. I decided I wanted to build an encryption algorithm for the science fair.

I used Turbo Pascal, an early programming language, to write an algorithm that would take inputted text and output encrypted gibberish. Anyone who understood encryption might know what was happening on the back end of the algorithm, but it wasn't theatrical enough to demonstrate at a science fair. So, I started thinking, *How am I going to sell this to my peers, the judges, the sponsors, etc.?* I realized I needed to make it easy for anyone to use—not just those who understood the software-development platform Turbo Pascal. So, I looked at the MS-DOS edit program (the early version of Microsoft Word) user interface and wrote a program that looked like that, with the ability to save, delete, copy, etc. Essentially, I developed a text editor. Then, I embedded the algorithm into that. Using a password, you could watch your text be encrypted through rotating key-cipher encryption as it happened. It was *fancy*, if I do say so myself, and I won my category at the science fair.

Next, I went on to the regional science fair in Baton Rouge. I remember setting up my Gateway 2000 on one of many tables lined up in a high school basketball gym. The judges and attendees loved my demo because they could experience it. They could input whatever they wanted and watch it encrypt and decrypt, like something out of a spy movie. I won the region and even won a graphing calculator from the U.S. Navy, which sent representatives to science fairs to recruit the next military whiz kids.

Next, I went to the Louisiana state science fair. I walked up and down the rows and saw someone else with an encryption program and thought, *Damn, that looks better than mine.* It was. He won first, but I won second. I received another navy science award, an army science award, cash, swag, and more. Even though I didn't win first place, this was a huge moment for me. I realized I could write code and people might pay me money for it. I experienced the rush of satisfaction in finding a need, selling a solution, and getting rewarded for it. Most entrepreneurs I know went through a similar epiphany that hooked them for life.

My lawn business had taught me the basics of running a business, getting customers, and minimizing debt. But this nerd had way too many allergies to build an outdoor business, and I was tired of sneezing through every job. Thanks to my science-fair success, I realized I wanted to make money with my mind, not with my muscles, so I shut down my lawn-service company. I was learning that my best business opportunities were likely within that computer.

My First Consulting Business

I chose to go to a particular public high school, High School for the Engineering Professions within the Scotlandville Magnet High School campus, in a rough part of my hometown of Baton Rouge, Louisiana, because it was an engineering high school. In 1980, the movie *Fame* came out, which was about a performing-arts high school. My high school was just like that, but instead of dancing in the hallways, it was comparing calculators and pocket protectors. It was *super* nerdy, *super* geeky, and all about science, technology, engineering, and math. We didn't have football, baseball, or basketball because the school thought too many sports would be a distraction—we did have track and soccer though. During lunchtime my entire freshman year, I played chess with my history teacher. We had a 100 percent high school graduation rate, and we had a near 100 percent college-graduation rate. Multiple students from my class had PhDs within a few years of graduating, and so many tech companies were started by graduates of that school.

It shouldn't surprise you that I was an enthusiastic member of our high school computer club, run by one of the best humans I know: Ron Dupuis, our computer science teacher. In the computer club, we built Gopher sites, which were like really lame versions of web pages today, but back then, we were pretty proud of ourselves. Before we had the internet and could build the Gopher sites, we built bulletin-board systems (BBS). These systems could connect you to other exchanges to post and retrieve communications and files. It was awesome. BBS systems were the social media sites of the early '90s—there were no influencers, photo filters, or emojis, just nerds talking to other remote nerds.

In 1995, Southern University, an historically black college and university (HBCU) down the road from our high school, chose to provide our school a free high-speed internet connection. They knew our school would make the most of it, and we absolutely did. Our computer club used the high-speed internet to start an internet service provider (ISP) for our parish (similar to a county in other states). We especially wanted to help our teachers who lived in the area get online from home.

While I was helping manage the ISP, we identified a major flaw in our plan. Teachers were calling because they didn't know how to connect and use their new, free internet. This was my first lesson in customer service—the more clients you have, the more support you need to provide. I realized there was a business opportunity here. It was hard back then to get on the internet. You had to have a dial-up modem, open phone line, internet service provider, the software to connect all those things, and a web browser, like Netscape. You had to connect and use them all to access the web. It was very complicated for most people, but I managed to grasp it pretty quickly since I had been experimenting with computers for five years already. I realized I could make a business out of helping teachers connect to the internet we were providing.

"Hi! Thanks for calling. I can come to your house, do all the setup, and teach you how to use your new internet for $40/hour. I'll have everything installed and configured, and you'll know how to use it." To my astonishment, most teachers replied, "Yes, please." It usually only took about two hours, and if for some reason I couldn't get it working, I didn't charge them. I remember my mom was floored at how much people were paying me—considering minimum wage was around $4.25 an hour in 1995. I called this hourly consulting business JB Consulting. (I know, I know, I didn't get creative with branding until many years later.)

A lesson I didn't expect to learn from this business came

from one simple fact: I didn't enjoy doing the work. While I love technology, I don't have a passion for internet services or hardware. I didn't love driving around town to people's houses. I loved writing code and building computer applications, but this consulting business made me good money, and I had very few expenses. I realized how profitable consulting services were and how they could fund whatever business I really wanted to build next. This lesson would later pay off in spades with JBKnowledge.

CHAPTER 4

SURVIVE
SO YOU CAN
THRIVE

W hen I was getting paid $40 an hour to help teach-
ers set up their internet connections, I definitely
had a few moments of thinking, *Maybe I don't need
college.* But no matter how pro-do-it-yourself my dad was,
he wouldn't let me entertain that idea. Dad was ardently

pro-college, and he knew what I wasn't mature enough to know at the time: I was self-limiting. I was too confident in my ability to "make it." I was making $40 an hour, nearly ten times the minimum wage that year, and I thought I was rich. For a seventeen-year-old, I *was* rich, but for an adult, I most certainly was not. I had no expenses and no rent, insurance, or loan payments. I needed the experience of being humbled by living costs and adapting to group environments.

There's a reason so many people refer to college as their "formative years." College is a giant incubator for, well, everything. Social skills, businesses, recreational activities, habits, addictions—the good and the bad. You're smashing a bunch of people together before they have to officially join the real world and after they've had some shelter from their families. They learn soft skills and hard skills. It's a (relatively) safe environment to experiment and explore what it means to be an adult and a professional.

While college is an incubator, it's not immune to the broader societal and economic changes happening off campus. I attended college from 1997 to 2002, and several monumental world events happened during that period. Y2K, the dot-com bubble bursting, and September 11th, to name a few. Words I had never used before became a part of my regular vocabulary: "boom," "bust," "dot com," and "terrorism," among others. Along with this new vocabulary came a new way of seeing the world in all its unpredictability.

For the first time, I understood what it would mean to graduate college, to leave the incubator, and become a truly independent adult responsible for my own future. It was an exhilarating and overwhelming thought and probably the reason I approached my final years in college intent on working for a large consulting firm that would give me a big salary and safety net. The idea of running my own "grownup" business seemed risky when you can never control all the variables. On the news and in my classrooms, I witnessed the timing, planning, perseverance, and, sometimes, luck a business needs to survive. I was considering if I was up for the challenge.

Learning Followership before Leadership

If you've met someone who went to Texas A&M University, you likely remember the encounter. Aggies like me aren't subtle. We are especially crazy about meeting other Aggies. We all wear these Aggie rings that date back to 1889. We say/ shout things like, "Gig 'em," and we have more than the usual number of collegiate hand signs. We "Whoop!" at seemingly random moments, and we worship these elected students in overalls called Yell Leaders. It's ridiculous and awesome at the same time.

Texas A&M is one of six public universities in the United States that has a Senior Military College, the volunteer Corps of Cadets. It's essentially the military college inside A&M. There are over two thousand cadets that live together, eat together, and sleep in dorm rooms known as barracks. Every day, they march into chow (mealtime) twice, perform two hours of drills, get into formation, and wear a uniform to class. While the service academies like West Point and the Air Force Academy can definitely claim to have more strict

The number one rule of business is to survive.

Above all else, you must stay in business long enough for good things to happen. This means making tough decisions that drive the long-term viability of the business, not short-term or unsustainable results.

and rigorous schedules, at least their cadets don't have to sit next to carefree college students in sweatpants every day, constantly reminding them of a breezier college experience. So in 1997, I started in the Corps of Cadets at Texas A&M, and I had no idea I'd be starting a business from my dorm room four years later.

I began my studies in the Computer Science Department, for obvious reasons. Because of my high school education, it started easy and unfortunately did not get much harder. After two years, I realized the department was behind the curriculum my STEM-focused high school had offered. I don't blame the university—the developments in technology, thanks to the internet, had far outpaced the process of getting new curricula approved. (I've mentored and taught students currently in the department, and it's now very competitive and current.) I decided if I couldn't get more computer science experience, I could get more business experience. I decided to pursue my undergraduate degree in accounting and my master of science in information systems instead. Through a program at Mays Business School, this would take five years total. I figured accounting would teach me the mechanics of business—how money moves and how to understand cash flow, taxation, debt, and assets. I also figured information systems would put my computer skills into the context of broader business systems and teach me how to harness data to fuel a business.

These degrees proved to be the right choice, but the real lesson came during my junior year in the Corps of Cadets. Throughout my freshman year, I did not impress the upperclassmen. As a result, when selecting our sophomore positions within our units, they designated me Weather Corporal. No, I didn't get to report the weather; instead, I got to work out every time it rained. It was a position given to the freshman they wanted to humble, and I can admit I needed it.

As a sophomore, I decided to pursue a better position on my own, and I found a junior-year cadet, Christian Beard, who was on the Corps Staff managing information technology for the entire Corps of Cadets. I told him what I could build and volunteered to help him in any way possible. He took me on as a protege of sorts, and when it came time at the end of my sophomore year to select a replacement for his position, Corps Staff selected me. I was an Information Management Sergeant during my junior year. The upperclassmen who had made me Weather Corporal were floored. The next year, my senior year, I was selected as the Information Management Officer—the lead technologist for the entire Corps. To go from Weather Corporal to a position on the Corps Staff—which only twenty cadets out of the entire two thousand were selected for every year—was a huge feat. They knew they'd underestimated me. Conversely, I knew what I'd do differently so that wouldn't happen again in the future.

I was assigned Weather Corporal because I did not understand that anyone who wants to lead in the Corps has to do so by example. I enjoyed my freshman year, maybe a little too much. I didn't work hard enough to show I could be a reliable, capable, and loyal leader of my peers. But when I was promoted to Corps Staff, I had to be beyond reproach 24/7 to keep my position. How I dressed, how I studied, how

I partied—it all mattered. Rank has its privileges, but it has even more responsibilities.

As the Corps' Information Management Officer, I led a team of roughly fourteen people, and there were over eighty individuals in my chain of command. One of my proudest accomplishments was building a system that took us paperless so we didn't have to have print memos, training schedules, and operation orders. We digitized that whole process, and I've been on a mission to eliminate paper-heavy processes ever since.

I learned how to issue orders, delegate tasks, and figure out what motivates people, which was especially important since we weren't being paid for our work. That was really my first leadership experience, and it was incredibly valuable. Not just because I was learning to lead, but because I was learning what it means to follow. For someone with my confidence, or *overconfidence*, that was critical. I may have had people "under" me, but there were far more people "over" me and even more people I was accountable to. A lot of leadership programs don't dive into followership; they jump straight into leadership. But not a military college. They teach you how to follow orders, obey orders, pass down orders, be part of a team, and strengthen the chain of command. I quickly learned the strength of a team versus the strength of one individual. Appropriately, the Corps motto is "Per Unitatem Vis"—through unity, strength.

I had no idea how critical these lessons in followership and unity would become as the new millennium approached.

The Chaos of 2001

One of the more interesting things to live through, technologically speaking, was the advent of the web and the first big asset bubble around technology, which occurred between 1993 and 1999. We had these brand-new technologies: the internet, websites, and mobile information. We knew they would radically reshape the way we live our everyday lives, and everyone speculated on how. Some venture capital firms speculated with billions of dollars' worth of investments in really bad ideas. Yes, some speculated on really great ideas, but most were unfortunately just way too early.

I was a computer geek and college student during this time, so I followed all these tech companies, like Pets.com, Webvan, and WorldCom, as they ramped up. At the same time, an unanticipated question was emerging: what would happen when the clock struck midnight on New Year's Day of the year 2000? The simple mistake of using two digits for the year instead of four in almost all computer systems caused most of the world to fear their systems were going to think it was the year 1900 instead of 2000. To prevent a massive systems failure, all software had to be upgraded. The companies providing upgrade services contributed to the ramp-up in tech investments in 1999. Fixing and solving all the Y2K compatibility issues had to be done—the demand was there. At the same time, the dot-com companies were absolutely exploding in valuation and dollars raised, but they weren't necessarily exploding in revenue or profit.

While the preventative measures taken to fix systems leading up to Y2K were successful, a handful of things still broke. (It's worth noting that Y2K was a non-event because smart people made it a non-event by spending and investing money to fix those systems, not because the predictions were wrong.) At the same time, investors were scrutinizing their technology investments due to the Y2K scare, and their appetite for companies that had little or no revenue had all but disappeared. The result was huge; publicly traded companies went bankrupt overnight. One of the most interesting companies that went bankrupt was Webvan. It was a grocery-delivery service pre-smartphones. In addition to taking on too much investment at too high a value with too little revenue, it was just too early to survive the year 2000.

The NASDAQ Composite Index bled over 40 percent of its value in 2000. From 1995 to 2000, at least three hundred companies went public each year. In 2001, only eighty had the heart and investors to do so. Despite this market chaos causing thousands of software developers to find themselves unemployed, some of those laid-off workers would go on to build startups like Facebook and Google. And those startups that managed to survive would soon become household names, like Amazon, IBM, and eBay.

Out of chaos was born a new beginning. So many tech companies started in the depths of this mini-recession, and a few survived and pivoted. Tech funding dried up, IPO valuations tanked, and public companies' stocks plummeted. The investor community said, "This isn't worth it." It created an enormous void in the market, or another way to look at it, an enormous opportunity for whatever could come next. At the same time, there was a huge economic crisis in Latin America, including Argentina, which would soon become a part of my story. There was a lot going on in the world.

Just before Y2K and the dot-com crash, I experienced chaos firsthand when the bonfire fell at Texas A&M. The first Aggie bonfire dates back to 1907, and over the years, it became a tradition to build the bonfire leading up to the Texas A&M versus University of Texas football game around Thanksgiving every year. The Corps of Cadets participated heavily in the building of the bonfire. It was a two-month process involving thousands of students and resulting in a five-story-tall stack of logs that was burned before game day. At 2:42 a.m. on November 18, 1999, the stack collapsed, and twelve Aggies were killed. Several of those Aggies were members of the Corps of Cadets. One of those cadets, Nathan Scott West, was from my outfit, C-2. We were working the bonfire that night, and I was supposed to be there. I'd accidentally fallen asleep with my bonfire clothes folded and ready at the base of my bed. As a member of the Corps Staff at the time, I was woken up and notified as soon as it happened, and our job was to account for every single cadet. Checking names off a list of people like that is something I never want to do again.

The bonfire collapse, Y2K, and the dot-com crash in March 2001 caused chaos and tragedy for so many lives and businesses. Unfortunately, the new millennium was just getting started.

As newly unemployed software developers and tech entrepreneurs picked up the pieces to rebuild the tech industry, September 11th, 2001, arrived, and with it, a reminder that tech, stocks, and employment only matter when we're free and safe to enjoy them. The American people, and our economy, took another gut punch we really couldn't afford. There was so much fear and anxiety generated from the fact that the United States and our financial capital of New York City could be so easily hit by a rogue terror organization. September 11th shook our economy and our identity as a country. I had traveled to New York City in August of 2001 to visit a former classmate working on Wall Street who I'd served on the Corps Staff with. I spent one afternoon at the top of the World Trade Center, and I will always remember how powerful the city felt from up there. I feel lucky to have that mental image from before the chaos.

Deciding to Be an Entrepreneur

Prior to September 11th and with Y2K looming, I was in my senior year, serving in my first official IT leadership position in the Corps and building relationships with the cadet alumni network. I discovered there were many former cadets who owned businesses and needed help with software. I started meeting with them and ended up contracting with my first for-profit client, American Lumber. Luckily, they were in an industry unaffected by the dot-com bust, so I met with their CEO, and he asked me to travel out to Uvalde, Texas, during my spring break in March 2001. He wanted me to write code to help perfect their inventory-management system—for $80 an hour.

High on cash flow right after that trip, I drove straight home to meet with my dad. I'd prepared spreadsheets of revenue and expense projections, lists of equipment I needed, and my business plan. I said, "I can build a software development business, but I need a little help getting started.

Here's what I need and how I'll pay you back." After poking sufficient holes in all my numbers, he said, "Let's do it," and wrote me a $5,000 check. The business was registered as JBKnowledge about a week later on April 16, 2001. We were up and running from my dorm room.

This didn't mean I'd decided to be an entrepreneur full time after graduation though. The last two years had taught me to be productively paranoid, so I continued to pursue corporate opportunities through my master's program, which began in the fall of 2001.

That fall, the business school took us on an educational trip to the Enron offices in Houston. We were shown what was said to be the pinnacle of capitalism. We toured the "Future of Energy Trading" at Enron, but it looked ironically like a dystopian future. The trading floors, beautifully built, were barely a quarter full with traders. I remember exiting one elevator, and there was a beautiful, custom motorcycle on display as artwork. On another floor, there were nearly three to four hundred workstations ready, and only two or three employees present. This was its bandwidth trading floor, and I remember thinking that as technology evolves, there will continue to be more and more excess bandwidth. I didn't understand how it would be successful enough to fill that floor.

Our professors were enamored by the company—and we in turn were learning to be. But by the end of the year, those professors would go from teaching Enron as the pinnacle of capitalism to teaching Enron as the poster child of corporate greed. To watch Enron go down in a giant ball of fire and take its accounting firm, Arthur Anderson, down with it was insane. It took years of court cases for Arthur Anderson to be cleared of all charges, but it couldn't survive the cost and publicity. It disintegrated as a firm, and the partners had to go to the other members of the Big Five accounting firms. Now, it's just the Big Four.

When I look at stories like Enron, MCI WorldCom, and Bernie Madoff, I don't believe that at the start of their careers they set out to commit mass fraud or be the case studies of corporate scandals. I don't think anyone begins their career saying, "I want to defraud a bunch of people and end up in prison for the rest of my life." I think what happened was they made small compromises along the way that accumulated. Maybe they missed a quarter on reporting and said, "Let's just fudge the numbers a little bit this quarter; it'll be fine. We'll make it up later." Or maybe they decided to forge *just one* financial statement to a client because they missed a promised return, and they didn't want to look bad. It only takes one wrong turn, and your destination has changed, along with your ETA. By the way, at the startup or small-business level, you'll run out of time much quicker than Enron did.

My dad used to say there were too many legitimate ways to make a dollar to try and do it the illegitimate ways. Enron and Arthur Anderson learned that you only sell your reputation once.

Through luck, and maybe some intuition, seeing Enron's offices didn't lure me into their world. While completing my master's program, I had my first internship with a large, global accounting firm. It went well, but it just didn't feel right. My internship manager even took me to the forty-first floor of this very tall building in downtown Dallas, and we looked out over all of Dallas and Fort Worth. At the time, roughly six or seven million people lived within that view. He offered me a full-time job upon graduation and gave me the blockbuster "This can all be yours" speech. He said I could be a partner there someday, and I just remember thinking, *No... there's got to be more than this. This can't be it.*

The offer dominated my thoughts for a week. When they called to ask if I was accepting the job, I declined, explaining that I needed to go out on my own and continue pursuing whatever JBKnowledge could be. "Plenty of people wanted this job," they replied. After all, this was fall of 2001; the world and the U.S. economy were still reeling from the September 11th terrorist attacks. I responded, "Well, then you won't have a problem filling it." While I'm usually a fan of burning the ships like Cortez did, in hindsight, this was not my best response. I've since learned it's okay to burn the ships but not your bridges. Once you make a decision, commit fully and trust yourself to move forward. But don't let your ego equate moving forward with forgetting the past—maintain relationships and paths that may be useful later. I'll never know if a relationship with that firm could have been useful. There was no going back after I said that. The conversation ended quickly. The position was filled, and then the economy crashed.

So, it's my fifth year, I'm back on campus, I had just completed two accounting internships and declined a job offer, and I've met some former cadets who have businesses and need help. I've registered a business and have a little capital from my new business partner, my dad. I get to lead a cool team of people that are digitizing the Corps, a two-thousand-person organization. I am motivated and in my element—a good place to be when making a risky decision.

I felt in my gut that there was no better time or place to pursue running my own business than right there in that dorm room. I knew I wouldn't have the same boldness once I was out in the business world earning a good salary. I was already used to eating ramen and mac and cheese, living in a small space and on a tight budget. In my mind, it was a short leap from college life to the life of a startup entrepreneur. This is something I tell students now frequently.

On paper, the Corps of Cadets doesn't look like a breeding ground for entrepreneurs, but if you look beneath the groupthink traditions of Texas A&M, you'll see how they break down the barriers you've drawn around yourself. It's no longer about you. It's about building on what came before you for those who will come after you—it's about the mission. The right mission can withstand an onslaught of chaos. Starting a business couldn't be more similar. Everything in your possession is on the table—your assets, your time, your relationships—but a business started with the right mission can survive.

While I've had time to reflect on all this since, it wasn't running through my mind the day I decided to forgo my goal of working for a multinational consulting firm to pursue the more exciting route of running my own business. That day, I was just another senior in the Corps of Cadets with $1,500 senior boots—the most expensive shoes I'll ever own—sitting in a tidy dorm room. That room housed the red Torelli road bike I'd bought after my internship. Swim gear from my stint on the TAMU club water polo team was tucked barely visible under the bed. I was sitting at my Gateway 2000 computer, one of a handful of Cadets to have a computer in their room AND know what to do with it, and I began mapping out on the whiteboard to my right a vision for a multi-hundred-person technology-development company. I'd watched the rise and fall of businesses, economies, and communities as if it were on fast forward from 1999 to 2001. I was motivated to build something amidst the chaos that could survive whatever chaos came next. Even better, my dad believed in my plan, and that's all the confidence I needed.

CHAPTER 5

CHOOSE PARTNERS WISELY

I n a startup, you end up making decisions based on the people you have. You don't have the budget to recruit the most experienced people, so you often hire based on personality, and then you trust them to learn and learn fast. Since startup founders tend to be learning on the fly, they aren't scared of letting others do the same. There's a monumental amount of trust put into early team members who wouldn't get the same treatment at larger organizations. Moreover, there's almost limitless opportunities for people to shape the future of a startup in those early days.

Your first hires are critical, especially considering they won't all stick around. You'll learn how to identify those that will, and it'll be a painful but worthwhile process. What you can't afford, though, is to choose *partners* who won't stick around, not if you're bootstrapping. By partners I mean anyone who has an equity stake in your business, like co-founders, investors, or advisors.

A common reason startups fail is because the founding leaders don't work as a partnership. Not because they aren't smart or talented enough, but because they don't have a (nearly) unconditional commitment to each other and to success, whatever that may evolve to look like. They don't commit to changing, growing, and becoming a new type of partnership every time the company needs it.

My dad and my COO, Sebastian Costa, are my most important partners. Not only because we spend the same amount of time together, but because they share my vision enough to dedicate their lives to it too.

It can be hard to find partners like this who aren't your co-founders—especially in the investment community—but it's worth your time to try. Every decision maker or source of funds you bring in can dictate your direction, shape your team, and, ultimately, impact the value you walk away with someday. It's important you trust them completely with your vision.

Choose your partners wisely.

Anyone who has an equity stake in your business should be chosen slowly and wisely. Alignment in your values and vision is more important than any dollar amount or business plan.

Why College Station?

The beautiful thing about living and starting a company in College Station, Texas, is that I am mere hours from more than fifteen million people. It takes less than three hours to drive to Dallas, Fort Worth, San Antonio, Austin, and Houston. I decided to build from this little town because of this three-hour distance to what is arguably the eighth- or ninth-largest economy on the planet.

Several years ago, a very close friend of mine was successfully bootstrapping a services business in College Station and wanted to build an app that would have a huge social impact. He planned to facilitate the flow of massive amounts of capital to organizations and nonprofits that desperately needed it. I couldn't believe that it didn't already exist—it was an awesome idea from an awesome guy.

His main business was a bootstrapped, cash-flow-positive services business building web applications and mobile apps for companies. He didn't love it, but it generated a profit and kept his team employed. With the profits, they began building this app product on the side but at some point decided, "We've got to go 100 percent all in on this app."

To them, that meant raising capital. They found angel investors and raised about $1.3 million in capital for their technology product. They then became convinced they had to move to run the company. So they left our "one-horse town" and went to the "big city" because that's where everyone said they should go. All tech companies go to Austin and get an expensive office—one that is about eight times more expensive than their old offices—and they get new everything. It's like "Keeping up with the Joneses"—startup style. I watched a plethora of irrational decisions get made while they were playing with OPM—Other People's Money. A big challenge within the venture-capital community is that they, knowingly or unknowingly, create OPM addicts. Once startups get that money, they spend in ways they likely never would have had they earned that money through profit-generating activities on a bootstrapping budget.

This is where I remind you the bootstrapping mindset is just as powerful for those who have raised money as those who choose not to. Simply put, capital-efficient companies have a better chance of surviving.

At the same time his company was moving to the big city, my friend was told by his investors that he had to bring in an outside CEO, and it was more of a demand than a suggestion. The CEO they brought in proceeded to go on a spending binge in order to "ramp up quickly." Half their investment capital was spent before they realized their business model required a significant pivot. Unfortunately, they hadn't reserved enough money to pivot, and they were out of business within about fourteen months. It was a matter of operations, timing, and investment philosophy that caused their downfall, not a bad idea.

So what does this story have to do with College Station, Texas, and why I've kept my company headquarters there since 2001? I believe one of my friend's biggest mistakes, other than bringing in someone other than the founder to be the CEO (more on that later), was believing he had to leave our small town for the big city. This significantly increased expenses without any direct correlation to increasing revenue. He was building an app, after all. Founders have been building and launching apps from garages all over the world for as long as we've known about the internet. With the mobility and remote accessibility of the workforce these days, where you headquarter your business can have a huge impact on your ability to bootstrap, minimize expenses, get profitable, and scale. You also need to build a business where you have room (physically and monetarily) to grow, not where you can barely afford the square footage your desk occupies.

My dad once told me, "Always have more office space than you need." Why? In case you need to grow quickly and to motivate you to grow. He told me, "James, it'll drive you crazy, which is a good thing. You'll walk around your office, and you'll try to figure out ways to fill that space up with productive activities and people." He was absolutely right. From the beginning, we always kept excess office capacity, and this was only possible because of the low facilities cost of being in a small town like College Station.

Another pro of starting a business in a small town that most people think is a con is in recruiting talent. While the pool of candidates may be smaller, there's another way to look at it. The tenure of our employees in College Station averages five years. You won't find many other tech startups with that kind of employee retention. They are poached and recruited by all the other big tech companies in a big city and rarely stay in one place for long. But we found if we spent the time to find the right fit for a role, we could hold onto them for long periods of time because we could offer them a role they couldn't find elsewhere in that small town.

On top of that, in our town we have this small, seventy-thousand-student university named Texas A&M. While most students are ready to get out of town by the time they graduate, they are all looking for internships while they're here. We figured out what on-campus jobs were paying and offered nearly double that per-hour rate. We went to the business and engineering schools and asked to speak to classes and set up at career fairs, offering a paid intern program. We offered semester or summer paid internships to start, with the opportunity to continue if it went well. Seventy-five percent of our interns loved working with us, and the feeling was mutual, so we'd retain them for years, throughout their studies, and we'd be incredibly flexible around their classes and exams. They'd get better experience than most internship programs and didn't have to leave town and take on a new lease and expenses in a big city for a summer or semester. As we grew, we'd occasionally have a full-time opportunity open up, and we'd already have an intern of two or three years who was graduating and could be a great fit. It has been an incredibly productive pipeline for us that also established a culture of young, eager professionals constantly learning and experimenting.

Not only was it great for the students, but our staff learned the joy of mentoring and teaching students at the college level—they are like sponges, eager to learn and understand everything new to them. As a manager, you can't ask for a better attitude. Students are in a really cool stage of life where they are finally taking action and responsibility for themselves and their careers. If you ask any of our staff who worked with our interns over the years, they will say it was incredibly fulfilling to work with young talent at that stage.

Since 2001, College Station has afforded us office space and a talent pool that no big city could replicate. It has allowed us to efficiently manage our budget and expand internationally with a similar "find the best small towns" attitude. The worldwide shift to remote work in early 2020 has only further solidified our strategy.

The Integrator

I'll admit that when I first hired Sebastian, I just knew I liked him and he could do what I needed. I liked the idea of practicing my Spanish with him and helping him work in the U.S. I honestly had no idea that one email would turn into a lifelong partnership and friendship that I get emotional just writing about.

Sebastian Costa came to the U.S. for his senior year of high school as an exchange student. He dreamed of studying in a big, shiny city in the United States and playing baseball. He played for the Argentinian national team throughout his childhood. In 1993, there was no social media or Google Maps, and so Sebastian had no idea what to expect when he was assigned to an engineering high school in LA. Before he figured out he was going to Baton Rouge, he thought LA meant Los Angeles, not Louisiana. He found out upon arrival the school had no baseball team. His host was Ron Dupuis, the computer science teacher at his high school, and nerds like me met at his host's house every week. He watched *Saved by the Bell* and *Wings* to learn better English and quickly made friends playing other sports. We passed each other in Ron's doorway occasionally as he'd leave to play basketball at a local court while the computer kids took over his house. I got the impression he didn't think much of us. He was a jock, and we were nerds, a typical high school dichotomy. Later, I learned we had rubbed off on Sebastian at least a little, and he'd gone on to get a computer science degree from Nicholls State University in Thibodaux, Louisiana.

Sebastian graduated from our high school in 1994, and I had no contact with him until May 2001. I had just registered my company, JBKnowledge, and called my high school computer science teacher, Ron, for guidance. Ron told me Sebastian had graduated from Nicholls State and was currently looking for work on a one-year work visa. Ron's endorsement was all I needed to hire him.

From: **Sebastian Costa** sebastiancosta@hotmail.com
Subject:
Date: May 24, 2001 at 5:57 PM
To: Jbenham@ureach.com

James,
   I spoke with Ron this weekend and he told me to contact you about some web programming. He said that you were going to spend a few days in Baton Rouge and I thought I might email you first and give you a call as soon as you get back to Texas. He didn't explain much about what you needed or anything else but I'm really interested in working with you. I have your card and I will call you as soon as posible. I will be moving in with Ron this weekend and will probably stay there for a while.

I hope to hear from you soon.

Sebastian

Get Your Private, Free E-mail from MSN Hotmail at http://www.hotmail.com.

Sebastian lived with Ron for the year and worked for me. I traveled to Baton Rouge often, but mostly, we communicated over email. There were no smartphones then, and we weren't tethered to chat tools. The pace of business was remarkably slower. After all, sometimes we had to build the scope for a new development project by going to the library and looking up code in books on software. We worked well together. He was calm, where I was excitable. I pushed the envelope on ideas, and he dug in to help me figure out how to make them happen.

In September of that year, the World Trade Center was attacked. Not only did it have a significant impact on our morale, culture, and economy, but it also had a significant impact on the United States visa policies. It became much more challenging to get a work visa. As a brand-new company, I didn't have the clout or money to help Sebastian stay beyond his one-year work visa.

I called Sebastian and said, "Here's the deal. I can't do a work visa for you, but you have two options. You can go back to Argentina and work for me from there, or I'll help you find a job with one of the big accounting firms" (they were recruiting a bunch of computer science graduates then).

He said he'd think about it and called me the next day.

"I want to keep working with you," he said the next morning.

Why? I thought. He had every reason to pursue a position at the big corporate firms and stay in the U.S. I was puzzled but excited. We were off to the races.

Sebastian moved back to Argentina. He took his computer—a fifty-pound, cathode-ray-tube (CRT) display and a fifty-pound tower—checked it in his baggage, and flew to Buenos Aires to set up his apartment for remote work.

Starting in 2002, one of my very close friends from high school was also working with us. At the time, we were halfway through three important projects. I noticed there were some problems with the projects and communication started to lag. I called Sebastian and said, "I think something's going on, but I'm not sure what the problem is." Sure enough, my friend sent me an email about a week later that said something like this:

Hey, I stopped working on this project two weeks ago. I'm sure you and Sebastian can figure it out. I'm leaving and moving towns. Good luck.

Not only had we already paid him for incomplete work, but we were unable to get valuable information from him before he left. I could hear my dad in the back of my head, "The number one rule of business is to survive, and only the paranoid survive." I had failed to be productively paranoid.

I had failed to "trust, but verify" with my team. I've since learned that people who do their job and do it well don't mind as long as you verify in a respectful way. Both the method and message matter. You have to be willing to hold even your best, most loyal people accountable for their performance. No matter what I told myself in 2002, this disaster didn't happen overnight. There were signs leading up to receiving this email that the employee wasn't on track, but I was avoiding holding him accountable and was instead just hoping he was getting things done.

On the day I received that painful email, I called Sebastian and said, "We have two choices. We can expand in Argentina, or we can shut down. If we want to stay in business, we're going to have to hire people outside the U.S. to get these projects done, or I have enough money to pay our clients back what they paid us for the contracted projects, and we can then move on independently and find jobs."

It wasn't really a choice for either of us. For the second time, he said, "Let's keep going," and I agreed. Argentina's exchange rate was going crazy because their currency had collapsed a few months earlier. We were able to take what we were paying one person in the U.S. and hire five in Argentina plus rent an office within three weeks in Salta, Sebastian's hometown, where we decided to set up our first office. There are probably five million bootstrapping lessons in that eighteen-month timeline I just gave you—from hiring Sebastian to moving into our Salta office. There's a quote that I particularly love from John Wooden that summarizes them all: "When opportunity knocks, it's too late to prepare."

Our working together really became a partnership when he agreed to build a team in Argentina. To him, it may have been just another adventure and chance to solve a new puzzle, but for me, it was a huge deal for him to say, "I'm in." Because he was really saying, "I'm in. We're going to do this internationally, and I'm going to help you figure this out. I believe in your vision, and I believe we can make it happen, even if we don't have an exact plan." Finding my co-founder felt a lot like proposing marriage. There was a mix of "Do you really like me this much?" and "Damn, are we sure?" and "This is so awesome."

In the Entrepreneurial Operating System, which I'll explain in more detail later, a company is led by a Visionary and an Integrator working in partnership. They are critical to the functioning and success of an organization. They aren't always equals or co-founders, but they are as close as you can get. The Visionary is exactly that—the one who sees the future of the company and what it should look like. They're often big-picture thinkers with big ideas, but they aren't great at execution. The Integrator is the opposite—they thrive on execution and determining the steps and pace needed to reach a vision laid before them. They take ideas and turn them into actions. A company cannot succeed without both.

This isn't groundbreaking—most companies have a CEO and a COO that work in tandem and have roles similar to what I described. The issue, though, is that these roles don't always have the trust to challenge each other, listen to each other, disagree with each other, and still get on the same page before moving forward. Another common issue is that one may covet the other's job, leading to jealousy based on who is executing what and who is in the spotlight. Knowing and communicating what you each want out of your roles as Visionary and Integrator are key before teaming up.

If you don't have a co-founder, that's okay, but you do need an Integrator as soon as you can find one. They'll help your vision follow a reasonable and budget-appropriate path so you don't run out of money before you arrive. Or maybe you're an Integrator and need to find a Visionary. Whether you're running a research project or a startup, this partnership is critical for innovation and building a sustainable effort. There's a common myth about needing an outside CEO, but most entrepreneurs I meet really just need an Integrator to execute their visions. I was lucky to meet the Integrator of a lifetime, Sebastian, right out of the gate.

The Yellow-Chair Phase

Those early days of establishing JBKnowledge were humbling, and I learned a lot of things the hard way. As I brought on Sebastian and our first international employees, my ego was learning what it really means to be a founder and a leader.

When I went to Argentina the very first time, I wanted a sign on our new office door that said "JBKnowledge, Texas, USA, Salta, Argentina," because it made me feel like an international businessman of mystery. So we put the sign up, and the week after I left, my employees took the sign down. My ego had made two main mistakes. First, I had put Texas before Argentina. Second, the sign disclosed we were Americans with expensive technology, which made us a target for theft. Thankfully, my team had my back. We haven't had signs outside our offices in Argentina since.

Next, my ego said, "Let's set our employees up on the top floor of this five-story office building in Salta because it has the best view of the mountains." Reality said, "You don't have air conditioning. Hope your employees, who grew up looking at those mountains, enjoy the sweat box."

I wasn't thinking about my company, my equipment, or, most importantly, my people. I was putting my ego first. In bootstrapping, you're limited on resources, so what you have is precious. Every employee willing to work for a below-market salary. Every office space you find that you can afford. The only way to maintain them long enough to get profitable, especially if you're trying to operate internationally, is to make decisions that prioritize those resources, not your ego. It also helps if you have a partner like Sebastian to call you and your ego out as needed.

Right now in 2022, if you were to travel to Argentina or any South American country, you could have a $10-a-day mobile-phone plan that would allow you to communicate fully with unlimited calls, texts, and data. When we first leased that office in Argentina in 2002, not only did we not have international mobile phones, but I had *just* gotten my first mobile phone in the U.S.

We didn't have high-speed broadband in our office, and we especially didn't have it in people's homes. We had to set up a 56K dial-up modem connection, and we had to have our first five employees share a dial-up modem because we couldn't even get a digital subscriber line (DSL) in our office. This was like trying to drink molasses through a coffee stirrer in winter. This was the pathetically slow connectivity on which we were building software applications and transferring them internationally.

Sebastian loves telling the story of how we interviewed our first employees in Argentina. We didn't have an office yet; his dad, who came to work for us, was working on that. But he did have a friend in town who was an orthodontist and had an extra exam room. That's where he conducted our first interviews. Sebastian also had his best friend sit in with him to make the process feel more official, but he didn't tell any of the candidates that his best friend had no background in technology or software. He was there to nod along and ask, "Can you elaborate on that?" and help Sebastian feel more comfortable. Sometimes, you have to fake it till you make it.

Sebastian had only been through one technical interview in his life during college. I had been through zero—having only done case study interviews for consulting companies. Because we didn't know what we should be asking or how to ask it, the interviews were pretty simple. We got to know the candidates as individuals and what they were looking for. Then we asked, "Do you think you can write code, and do you own a computer?" We couldn't afford to buy computers for them initially and needed them to bring their own. Two of our first hires, who are vice presidents at the company today, will tell you they thought the whole thing might be a scam to steal computers. We joked about (but seriously considered) putting the Argentinian equivalent of "BYOC" on the job descriptions.

Sebastian's uncle was gracious enough to donate some very old, very used training desks to our first Argentina office from a local IBM training center he previously ran. They were small and uncomfortable training desks with small and uncomfortable yellow plastic chairs. We were working for six clients in the U.S. I was in the U.S. selling. The Argentinian office, led by Sebastian, was delivering the development product from an office with painful yellow chairs, no air conditioning, and a shared dial-up modem connected to employees' personal computers. It was all we could afford, and it bonded those early team members, many of whom are on our company leadership team today.

We often say to each other, "No one will understand our yellow chairs." We can't expect future staff to "get it" like our early team did. We can't expect future clients to understand where we started. No matter how many books you write or speeches you give about your bootstrapping experience, no one will understand what you went through to build your business. What matters is you've carefully chosen partners along the way who are willing to struggle and survive alongside you.

CHAPTER 6

CHIEF EVANGELIZING OFFICER

O ver the years, I've served as an adjunct professor at Texas A&M—the university just couldn't get rid of me. I've lectured to students in the construction science, business, and computer science departments, and they always want to know *how* to identify the next great business opportunity. They want to understand how to identify what they should build, for whom, and why. While these are important questions, I often remind them that building is only half the battle. If a product is built and nobody is hustling it at a tradeshow, did that product ever really exist? Developing a product doesn't make you a product company. People have to be marketed and sold to. They have to be supported and upsold. The early years of JBKnowledge drilled this into me.

In the early years of running a startup, I learned it's okay to not fully understand where your company is going to take you—in fact, it's better you're not married to one product, service, or industry at the beginning. It's better to see where and when opportunity emerges so you can find a valuable niche. The beauty of bootstrapping is you can pivot to what's most profitable without having to run decisions by too many stakeholders. Sometimes, you have the product or service right but not the market; sometimes, it's the opposite. Sometimes, all you have is the right people, and you pivot until you nail the offering and market.

It took us three years of selling software-development services to advertising agencies before we found our first real service niche in insurance. It took us five years and five failed software products before we found our first real product niche in construction. The only reason we arrived at either of those was because we focused on selling. If we couldn't sell something, we tried harder. If we still couldn't sell something, we pivoted.

I learned it was critical for me to lead that sales effort—if the guy with the vision and all his assets on the line wasn't going to get out there and sell, how could I expect my team to?

PRINCIPLE:

Get out and sell.

If you want to build
your vision, you have to be
the Chief Spokesperson.
No one else is going to
have the drive to build
your dream for you.

Our Most Profitable Industry

Our first four years in business weren't amazing. We were scrambling to find our niche, and I didn't understand marketing or advertising, that is, building a pipeline of people who come to you for work. But with payroll and my personal assets on the line, I was definitely motivated to get out and sell. At one point, I drove around Texas from Tuesday through Thursday every week. I'd learned from my dad's strategy of building his Teflon business, and I researched local businesses in each city's phone-book listings. I'd make a list and show up at an office to pitch what we could do. It was true "cold" calling, and it worked.

After my first time showing up and cold pitching to an advertising agency, something clicked. I realized they knew a ton about marketing, public relations (PR), and advertising (things I wanted to learn about) and were in charge of getting companies an online presence, but they knew nothing about the nuts and bolts of website development.

I adjusted my phone-book search to find more ad agencies. I'd walk in and ask if we could help them develop websites for clients, and surprisingly, many said yes. It was perfect timing because they had an explosion of need for website development but not enough web developers they trusted to get it done. They especially didn't know how to hire them in-house yet. It all started with a simple decision to get out and sell.

With every pitch meeting, I was learning to ask every prospect three direct questions that I still use today:

1. **Can I work for you?** ASK for the sale explicitly.

2. **Do you know anyone else I can work for?** ASK for a referral—they are often the strongest lead sources.

3. **Should I be a part of any trade associations you belong to?** ASK what organizations and events you should be networking and speaking at.

From asking the third question, I quickly learned that all the advertising clients I had signed were a part of the

American Advertising Federation (AAF). So I started attending all the regional meetings of AAF I could get to and signed more clients. They weren't dream clients. They were creative and inspiring to work with, but they didn't understand web development. They didn't always pay on time, but they were paying customers who kept JBKnowledge in business.

While networking and cold calling were having a positive effect, I realized I needed to build more recognition around my name and the company's brand to shorten the sales cycle. Because neither I nor JBKnowledge was a well-known name, I had to spend a good chunk of time establishing credibility and pitching my experience to every new prospect. From watching other business owners, I figured there were two ways I could do this: write a book or become a public speaker. Since this is my first book, you can guess which route I chose. You couldn't pay me to shut up about things I was passionate about, so speaking was a logical fit.

I was at an AAF Regional meeting in 2004 when I met a University of Texas grad through football banter. He was the Chair of the Florida/Caribbean Chapter. I asked him how I could go about getting a speaking gig in front of an AAF chapter, and he offered to give me a shot at upcoming meetings in St. Croix and St. Thomas. He even said they'd pay my expenses. Not a bad first gig.

This presentation forced me to spend time developing my speaking style and mantra, one that I still preach today: entertain, educate, and then, in the LAST minute, sell. (I'm incredibly proud to say that my twelve-year-old daughter recently put together a fifteen-slide deck to pitch me getting her the paid version of the Headspace app. She followed my mantra like a pro, presented her pitch, and got the sale!)

So, in 2004, I developed my first speaking presentation: "Outsource vs. In-House: How Do You Decide?" I delivered it to twenty to thirty attendees in a restaurant in St. Thomas overlooking the Caribbean Sea. Then I hopped on a seaplane and delivered it again in another picturesque restaurant on the beach at a resort in St. Croix. Ad agencies know how to promote their events, so they had local news there, and they interviewed me. I watched myself on the evening news from the hotel bar that night, toasting myself with a tropical drink. I was hooked on speaking.

Being a bootstrapped founder is exhausting and relentless. It feels like a long game of delayed satisfaction. But there are moments like this, when someone opens a door (or a seaplane) to you that you barely deserve, and the whole world presents itself to you as one giant opportunity. Those days, like this day for me in the Caribbean, are enough to last you months until the next magical moment. Part of the bootstrapping process is trusting those moments will come and hanging on long enough to experience them.

That trip was the beginning of my time speaking at most of the AAF chapters and regional events across the U.S., which generated over thirty clients for my fledgling company. I refined my speaking skills, networked like a maniac, satisfied my love of travel, and learned this industry we were now serving deeply. I was able to get my travel expenses covered, and after I'd built up some credibility, I was able to charge decent speaking fees on top of that.

As promising as this all sounds, ad agencies were not a

glimpse into our future but more a stepping-stone to it. I was experiencing the same feelings about working with ad agencies that I experienced about my high school consulting business—it could pay the bills, but I didn't want to do it forever.

I kept looking and cultivating referral sources outside of just advertising. I was referred to an insurance inspection company up in North Texas that provided an opportunity to bid on a software-development project. We bid, won, built it, and learned a lot about the insurance industry in the process. I realized that insurance companies were going to be around a long time, had a lot of cash, and were going to have increasing technology needs. I had a feeling that I had never had with my advertising clients: I thought, *We've got to go all-in on insurance.* That was a seminal moment. To this day, we specialize in and are known for our insurance technology products and services.

Offering Services versus Products

A big part of our success in the short term and long term as a company has been our structure as a services *and* products company. It's not common for companies, especially bootstrapped companies, to do both and do them well. The goal of most software companies, even if you start with development services, is to pivot into products as soon as you can. It's predictable revenue; it's not tied to your time; it "makes money while you sleep," as they say; and it's much easier to get a product company acquired or sold.

But we started JBKnowledge with the goal of retiring with the company—we weren't focused on a big exit or sale. Sebastian and I discussed this early on, and we told our employees that too. We made decisions about our business model that would optimize the longevity of the team. We never had an exit as our primary goal for starting the business, and ironically, that made our first product exit that much more interesting.

Offering technology-development services was a great cash-flow opportunity, especially in the early years of the company, when there wasn't a ton of competition and companies really didn't understand what we did. We had minimum expenses and overhead and were profitable almost immediately. I always wanted to build software products, though, and we learned that providing services gave us a lot of insight into the marketplace as to where there could be a need for products.

Once we started developing products, we discovered the expenses in labor, hardware, and software it required. Those expenses may run for twelve to twenty-four months before you onboard enough users to even get close to breaking even. Then, as you onboard users, you have new expenses to address, like user support, account management, new-feature development, and client retention. Building our first product taught us that if we wanted to keep bootstrapping, we'd need to maintain our services cash flow to subsidize product development. When we realized one could fund the other, we decided we'd always do both. While we shut down our first few attempts at a product, we kept trying and eventually got it right.

A big factor helping us maintain this structure of building products and services all these years, and figuring it out as we go, is people. People are the game-changer in so many parts of my bootstrapping story. Three of our first hires in Argentina now run our three biggest departments—Product Development, Software Development Services, and Design (the UX/UI, graphic, and web design team that supports the first two divisions). They started as the only people in their departments, but they each came from entrepreneurial backgrounds. Diego Heinrich, our VP of Product Development, owned and operated a private postal service before we found him in the middle of getting his computer science degree. German Maurino, our VP of Insurance Services, owned an internet cafe before he came to help us develop custom software for clients. Pablo Landriel, our Creative Director, worked for himself as a freelance designer before he came onboard to help us design our first interfaces and website. Our first HR, finance, customer service, and IT hires in the U.S. are still today our HR Director, Gabriela Salles; Finance Director, Jennifer Heninger; Customer Experience Director, Mark Fly; and Director of Architecture, Mike Bentley.

Our leadership team wants to retire with this business, and I know what a rarity that is. I also know the value it brings to our business having tenure in leadership. We have leaders willing to build great products and sell them but who also want to keep working together until we're old.

If you're a bootstrapper building a product company with an exit in mind, you can still be successful, but you have to acknowledge how that goal affects your mindset and those who work for you. Learn to talk and be transparent about it. Learn to set long-term goals and short-term motivations that keep people engaged and interested, even if they are working toward an exit. If you find the ultimate team, consider the route whereby you can offer services, sell off products, and keep your company and team operating, if that's something you're interested in.

Service companies don't build nearly as much equity value as product companies because their future revenue streams aren't predictable enough to drive high valuations—but they often have much better cash flow. The hybrid model we chose to pursue serves us, and our team, well. We have a services division that delivers consistent profit every year and a products division that doesn't generate a large profit but grows in value and equity.

Our Most Successful Failed Product

I've developed over fifteen software products since I learned to code at age eleven (and that doesn't include the custom products we've developed for clients). Some were experimental, some were failures, and some were wildly successful, but I strongly believe you can't get to that last category without the first two.

In the early 2000s, the more we provided software-development services, the more I wanted to be a software product company. I knew we could build value at scale with a product. With services, we would always be limited by hiring costs and the hours in a day. So we started identifying opportunities to build products in the services we were providing.

Working with so many ad agencies, we quickly realized

they needed better systems to run their companies. Most importantly, they needed to track projects, time, and expenses in order to bill each client. We developed the minimum viable product (MVP) of an agency management system (AMS) and started pitching it to clients. We knew they needed it and thought it'd be an easy sell. Turns out, they didn't see the need that their vendors and clients saw—they felt their systems were sufficient.

In addition to time and expense tracking, we also built a print-bidding feature into AMS. On top of building their websites, our design team helped a few of our ad agency clients with graphic design work. (Like I said, we took any job to feel it out!) We designed sign and flier graphics and had to figure out the best printing prices in town. We realized we could build a bidding module into AMS that let us send out the printing project to multiple printers and let them come back with estimates so we could pick one. It worked well for us, so we went back to our ad agency clients and said, "Okay, so you don't need the full AMS, but check out this bidding module." Again, they said, "No, thanks."

What we considered brilliant ideas turned out to be us chasing rabbits. My family and I are animal lovers and we rescue a lot of animals. We have eleven animals as I write this, and two of them are rabbits. They are total punks and incurably finicky. They never move in a straight line, they stop when they should go, and if you try to chase one, you end up looking pretty dumb.

As a bootstrapped entrepreneur, I was learning that you can't chase rabbits. You have to toe the line between quick pivoting through decisive action and erratically running off the trail into the woods. A lot of ideas sound like great ideas until you consider that everything's a trade- off and only the paranoid survive. Since the number one rule of business is to survive, you can't chase rabbits.

No matter how strongly I believed the AMS product was needed, the end user didn't feel the same, and we failed to find that out before building it. This was my first serious lesson in building a solution to a known, quantifiable problem, not a solution in search of a problem. There must be product-market fit.

I stopped pitching our AMS product to ad agencies, but I kept talking about it. I kept networking and speaking and traveling, and everywhere I went, I talked about what we'd built. I shared the experience to learn more from it and because I had this combination of code that I thought was pretty great. When you spend time and money on a product, even a "failed" one, you should talk about it. You never know what people are going to say and what ideas or introductions they're going to give you. So, I was talking about the product. My father was talking about the product. As a result, we met a friend of my father who said, "Hey, look, that print-bidding product would actually be really good for the construction market." And that was the beginning of our most successful product, SmartBid.

Opportunities in a Down Market

In the construction industry, for any new build or renovation project, there are generally four categories of companies involved after the architect and engineer: owners/developers (the ones with the money), general contractors (the ones with broad expertise and project management experience), subcontractors (the specialized companies with specific expertise, like painting, roofing, and plumbing), and suppliers (the companies that supply all the materials and parts needed by the subcontractors). When any new construction project is proposed, owners/developers send out the details of the project and invite general contractors to bid on it. In order to compile their bids, general contractors have to gather estimates from all the subcontractors and suppliers they'd like to use on the project. The most efficient way to manage this process is by using construction-bidding software. The software is usually purchased by the general contractor, who gives subcontractors and suppliers web-based access to view the project blueprints and submit their estimates. We learned that the workflow in construction-bidding software is surprisingly similar to how we would send a request for bids to printing companies via our AMS product.

In 2006, the leading software as a service (SaaS) provider in the construction market, iSqFt, acquired a bidding software called BidFax, a legacy DOS- and Windows-based faxing system that was the granddaddy product in the market. What I gathered from talking to a bunch of people (because I knew *nothing* about construction yet) was that iSqFt decided to shelve any updates on BidFax and encouraged users to switch over to the iSqFt platform. As you can imagine, the BidFax customers were not happy about this. They really wanted to continue to use their existing product. It was old, but it was familiar. I've been reminded of this many times over the years: just because a product is old doesn't mean people don't love it. There's a lot of value in the familiar. The BidFax users knew how to operate that system. They were construction professionals, not technologists, so learning how to use software was half the battle, and they didn't want to fight that battle again. They were understandably upset.

One of those BidFax customers was Mapp Construction, a general contractor in Baton Rouge, Louisiana. My father's friend knew the team at Mapp and introduced us to them. He said, "Hey, these people at Mapp, they were on BidFax, but they're not really happy about this migration and transition." He told us they were frustrated and might be open to looking at this bidding software we'd built for printing companies. He set up a meeting between us and Mapp. They said, "If you make these changes to this product, we'll consider using it." So we made about forty changes to the product, and in January of 2007, we went live with Mapp's Dallas office.

You're expecting me to say we found the perfect product-market fit and scaled quickly from there, right? Not quite. We onboarded eight clients in 2007 and thirty-two in 2008—not a huge growth rate, and here's why.

The beginnings of SmartBid, the SaaS product that would change my life, taught me the value of talking and timing. Talking about what you're working on until someone makes the connection you need. Timing of opportunities in mergers and acquisitions (M&A) activity and the economy. The timing to validate SmartBid in the construction market was right. The timing to really sell SmartBid to the construction market was not. The iSqFt acquisition was creating a shift among a big customer base, but the construction market was incredibly hot at the time. When the construction industry is hot, there are a lot of construction projects in demand to meet the supply of subcontractors. With fewer subcontractors bidding on each project, people didn't really need bidding software to collect and compare bids. They'd negotiate and award construction contracts directly. SmartBid was a great alternative to BidFax or iSqFt, but many people weren't convinced they needed a bid software at all because business was so good in 2007.

Enter September 2008: Lehman Brothers collapsed and the entire U.S. economy cratered in the Great Recession. When the global financial crisis occurred, construction companies that previously said they didn't need bidding software came back and said, "The work's all dried up. We have to bid now, and we need software." We learned that all the talking we had done about the product had paid off when the timing was right. They remembered us when they were ready to buy. I learned that a down market can be a fortuitous time to introduce a new product.

When times are really good, companies tend to lever up. They take advantage of low interest rates and available capital, and they take on debt. They use debt to buy buildings and expand. They use debt to buy other companies. When a financial downturn hits, like what happened in 2007, 2008, and 2009, their debt crushes them. They have to reduce staff. They have to shed some of their most expensive people, who also tend to be the highest performers. People drop out of the market. Some companies can't shed enough debt and go out of business. While these all sound like terrible buying signals for selling a product, we found a market demand that was actually inversely correlated with a good economy. When the economy worsened, construction-bidding activity went up, and people needed tools like software to support that surge.

Look ahead to 2021. We saw so many companies emerge from the turmoil of the COVID-19 pandemic successful because people stuck at home had an increased need for them—from grocery-delivery apps to leisure wear to eLearning platforms. (Imagine if Webvan had made it through 2000.) SmartBid taught me to look at each type of economic activity as an opportunity. "One man's trash is another man's treasure," as they say. It also reinforced another principle: "Get out, and stay out, of debt."

In 2007, just before SmartBid took off in 2008, we followed our own advice and paid off all the debt we had. I had credit card debt from starting the company and had taken on personal debt to supplement that. For example, I had to get a loan to buy the reliable Honda I drove around to generate business in the state of Texas. I had to use credit card debt to pay bills when I couldn't pay myself. Just before the recession, we paid all that debt off.

As a result, we entered the global financial crisis with more free cash flow because we didn't have any personal or corporate debt payments. At the same time, a bunch of talent came on the market because those companies that used leverage to buy out other companies and acquire them started laying people off. Those were really good people who were willing to work for less money. We picked up some incredible software salespeople who were pivotal to our growth and the growth of SmartBid in particular. They were laid off from their previous companies, sometimes our competitor companies, and came with their own connections and deep industry knowledge that they could share with me and our team. As long as we were willing to retrain them to our way of doing things, they were more valuable than hiring cheaper, less experienced salespeople who would take six months to build a reputation in the industry. At the same time, companies became interested in our bidding software as construction bidding ramped up. When we stepped back and stopped freaking out about the down market, we saw it had given us the gifts of cash flow, product demand, and talent. SmartBid's origin story taught me the importance of not only studying the industry you work in but also understanding the greater economic forces impacting that industry and how they can work to your advantage.

Working the Problem

Before we had our epiphany about how the 2008 down market could work for us, there was January 14th, 2008—a day I'll never forget. I remember sitting on the sidewalk outside our first College Station office and sobbing. I just lost it. I thought, *It's done. Everything I've worked so hard for is over.*

I had hired a college friend, and he managed our servers and performed hardware and software support for our team and clients. While working for me, he started a business on the side and neglected several of his duties. As a result, servers collapsed, and we lost five days of customer data. Our fledgling software, SmartBid, was down, and if you know anything about SaaS, you know the WORST thing that can happen is downtime—especially in the first year of building a product.

I called my dad first. He answered—he always does—and said, "James, first, calm down. It's okay. I'm here. Sebastian is here, we're here for you. Secondly, what can you do?" he asked. When I said I didn't know, he replied, "No, calm down. You're having a bad day, that's true, but stop feeling sorry for yourself. What can you do? What task can you do right now at this moment? What can you do that will start to make this situation better?"

I said, "Well, I can call all our customers and apologize. And ask them to give me a little bit of grace and offer some refund credits."

"Okay. Go do that, and then call me back," he replied.

Something he told me several times that day and hundreds of times throughout my life is "Work the problem. It's just a problem. What can you do next?" When stuff hits the fan and you're in crisis-management mode, you don't have time to wallow in how you got there or how to avoid it in the future; you have to focus on working the problem. Take one step at a time to remedy the existing situation, and reflect on it later with a clear head.

So I called each of our product customers and explained that we'd lost five days of data and begged them not to leave. Then I called roughly seventy hosting clients. It took me the whole day, as you can imagine. I called every single customer. I profusely apologized. I begged them for forgiveness, and I handed out tens of thousands of dollars in service credits.

How did they respond?

We didn't lose a single customer.

Nobody left.

In fact, they were supportive because I called them directly and honestly laid it all out. Many of them I had pitched and onboarded myself. As the Chief Evangelist of this little startup, they knew me well. I did not tell them about my baggage with the employee or try to escape blame—I told them that we lost their data, how that impacted them, and how I was going to make it right. They forgave us and stayed with us. It was amazing. If you're one of those clients and you're reading this, I hope you know how you impacted my life that day. That was the closest I've ever come to being completely and utterly bankrupt.

The Quickest Way to Learn a New Industry

I've learned there are very few mediums in life that allow you to have a broad level of influence over popular thinking and industries, to literally move large groups of people to take action on a shared passion. Social media, writing for print and digital publications, and events are a few of those channels, but the one I fell in love with was public speaking. I love the responsibility it demands to learn your audience, know what you're talking about, bring a unique perspective to a topic, and, ultimately, influence people to action. It's a responsibility I genuinely enjoy and revere.

As an entrepreneur, it feels hard to pivot industries because you develop a follower base within a particular industry, garner a reputation for certain thought leadership, and have a known resume. I had been speaking to dozens of ad-agency federations from 2004 to 2008 and had dozens more as clients. I knew we didn't want to do that forever, but we hadn't found a clear path out yet through our insurance clients. I had really crafted my message and thought leadership around the advertising audience. I had spent years and dozens of events talking to ad people in roles of all kinds about what they did, the challenges they faced, and how technology could help.

In 2008, when we began exploring the construction market for our bidding software, I realized speaking engagements could be my quickest way to not only learn the industry but establish myself in it.

As I started meeting with bid coordinators, estimators, and preconstruction managers at general contractors in the Southwest, to talk about this software we'd built, I'd ask, "Should I be a part of any trade associations you belong to?" The American Society of Professional Estimating (ASPE) was my first foot in the door and helped me meet the professionals managing construction bidding across the country. I asked member companies if I could visit their offices after presenting, and I'd sit next to them to watch their entire bidding process and understand how our software could improve it. Through those speaking events and office visits, I saw an industry that was ripe for change and disruption.

I started traveling around the country, speaking for free

at ASPE chapters and even covering my own expenses. I went from getting paid by advertising organizations to speak to having to establish my speaking credibility from the ground up in the construction industry. I had to push reset, and as you can imagine, it was very humbling for me. I can honestly say I spoke to almost every single ASPE chapter in the U.S. It was hard for them to turn down a free speaker. Through those trips, I spent hundreds, possibly thousands, of hours with estimators, learning their bidding processes, learning their pain points, and developing software to address them. I was determined not to chase any more rabbits.

Over the lifetime of our construction-bidding software, I went from having no SmartBid clients at each speaking presentation to having most of the people in the room as SmartBid clients. I also met and recruited many of my new team members. It started just by offering to speak, getting to know people, building a network, and not being stingy with conversations at events. I offered free advice whenever I could to show my technology expertise. Before long, I had developed a reputation as a speaker and technologist in construction. And our product was taking off because it actually addressed the pain points of users. After all, it was built from their feedback.

Had I not been willing to speak, travel, and network my way in, the construction business would have been way more daunting to penetrate. It's one of the oldest industries on the planet—the average company age is over twenty years. In the early 2000s, they hadn't ever heard the word "startup," and they weren't too sure about technologists—if the Empire State Building was built without the internet, why would they need SaaS?

You've likely heard the popular saying, "Give me six hours to chop down a tree, and I will spend the first four sharpening the ax." Regardless of your business model, as the saying goes, if you're going to work on solving a problem, spend fifty-five minutes of every hour studying the problem and five minutes designing the solution. When we pivoted to construction, I spent 95 percent of my time in construction offices and speaking to organizations, looking at where all their problems were.

The most insane process I saw involved architects getting plans to general contractors who then measured the plans for the owners, who had hired the architects. The architect would send AutoCAD files to a printer, who'd print the files out. The printer would then deliver the paper files to a general contractor. The general contractor would hand them back to the printer and say, "Scan it, and send me the PDF." UPS and FedEx had huge business lines shipping construction plans. There was so much wasted communication, shipping, and printing to produce a (heavy) PDF file that the architect had from the beginning and could have just sent to the general contractor if they'd had the means. It was an insane process, and I never would have understood it had I not spent a large amount of time in the field watching it happen. I wouldn't have believed it if I hadn't seen it.

My speaking engagements allowed us to learn, network, and pivot at a rate I don't think would have been possible otherwise in an industry ripe for change but averse to it.

Speaking allowed me to see the construction industry's reluctance as an opportunity to educate versus a barrier to entry. And the best part? Speaking is a great strategy for bootstrappers. If you focus on an area within driving distance, you can minimize expenses, and the main cost is your time. It's a "free" way to build exposure, get feedback, learn your industry, and embrace being your company's Chief Evangelizing Officer. Remember, "Entertain, educate, and then, in the last minute, sell." Speakers who just sell don't get invited back.

James's high school yearbook photo

Sebastian's high school yearbook photo

James marching in with the Texas A&M Corps of Cadets

Corps dorm room where JBKnowledge started with the first computer

James with his dad, Jim, at James's final review in the Corps of Cadets

Early days of James and Sebastian working together

Free but uncomfortable yellow chairs from the first office in Argentina

James speaking on stage at a conference in Canada

First Argentina office in 2002 with Sebastian, James, and their respective fathers, Ricardo and Jim

Most of the leadership team at the third and current office in Salta, Argentina during construction

The second office in Argentina with the full team

Early JBKnowledge leadership team

James and his dad, Jim, winning one of their first Aggie 100 awards

First research and development project with virtual reality (VR) in Bryan, Texas

James hosting The ConTechCrew podcast with Mike Rowe as the guest

Early days of the team meeting with clients in Argentina

Texas Southern University, where James serves as a Regent on the board

James doing what he loves: flying his plane

James with his dad in front of the airplane that his dad flew to Australia

James and Sebastian on the golf course at the 2022 Masters

CHAPTER 7

VALUES FIRST, VALUES SECOND, VALUES THIRD

Finding product-market fit for SmartBid and realizing our insurance technology services could fund our product efforts indefinitely kicked things into high gear for us around 2010. We'd had high growth year after year prior to that, but that's when we started to really embrace and push the growth.

That year, Sebastian and I met with another business owner in Vegas who had a professional services company in the construction industry, a self-described "lifestyle business." This meant he was building a steady-growth business that he didn't intend to sell. Instead, he built sustainable operations that made his team want to stick around a long time while supporting the lifestyle they wanted. He wanted to retire with his business like we did. He also wanted to buy SmartBid from us.

We were surprised. We were only four years into the product, and he thought it was worth buying from us. We declined but left the conversation with two main thoughts: 1) we have to invest in this product and think bigger if other people find it this valuable; 2) just because we want to build a lifestyle business doesn't mean we can't sell products off and keep the core business.

That year, we decided to commit to the construction and insurance industries wholeheartedly. We decided to let go of any clients not in those industries, sunset any services or products that didn't serve them, and adjust our marketing to target them. For entrepreneurs who like to pivot and keep their options open, this was terrifying. It was also really, really hard. We made a big decision with a quickly growing, international team.

Over the next several years, we'd face every growing pain of that decision. In 2017, it felt like we were finally on the other side, and I'll never forget the leadership meeting where we first seriously discussed selling our flagship product, SmartBid. Of the leadership team in the room, 90 percent had been there at the product's conception, and it was an emotional discussion.

Sebastian let everyone express their concerns, and then he said, "This is a big decision, and it's a hard decision. But at the end of the day, it's a great move for the company, and we're committed to keeping as many people as possible at the company who want to stay. And you know what, we can go build boats if we want to. I really believe this leadership team can do anything."

"We can build boats if we want to" has since become a well-known maxim at JBKnowledge.

Several of the people on that leadership team had zero relevant experience when they started at JBKnowledge. We just liked them, and we learned to spend most of our early interviews learning about the candidates as individuals—what motivated them, what they stood for, and where they wanted to go in life. We figured for the right person with the right values, we could find the right role as we grew.

From 2010 to that meeting in 2017, we scaled fast, broke a lot of things, and put the company back together stronger than ever. We learned how to stick to our values even when everything else got muddy, and the team that could build boats made it through to the other side.

You Can't Fight Culture

While we minimized the costs of growing by having operations in Argentina, we dealt with other challenges—like currency exchange rates, political turmoil, taxation laws,

Be willing to rewrite your rules but not your values.

Values must be known by all, followed by all, and used in every corner of the business; they should not be subject to ready change. Company rules, conversely, must be flexible enough to adapt to shifting cultures, changing operations, and innovation.

language barriers, and cultural differences. The way I had to learn to do business in Argentina was completely different from the way I had to learn to do business in the United States.

Whether you're looking to outsource your manufacturing, establish a customer-service center in a new time zone, or hire a development team offshore, I'd say the primary factor to consider is culture. Businesses too often consider this only after operations have commenced—they learn the quirks of the local culture and the communication differences they didn't know once the new line of business in a foreign country is up and running. Sometimes, these seemingly small differences can have huge impacts on the success of the company. When you're bootstrapping, all factors have to be considered thoroughly and quickly.

A small example of cultural differences at JBKnowledge is that when employees arrive at our Argentina office, they greet every single person. Every person gets a "Buen dia!" and a kiss on the cheek. Depending on when you arrive, this can become a twenty- to thirty-minute process. It's a necessary part of human interaction in their culture. In the later years of the company, when Sebastian, our Argentine COO, started spending more time in our U.S. office, he couldn't believe how many employees arrived and left without saying a word to him and their coworkers. Our U.S. staff has learned to get better at greetings and goodbyes, but it's a deeply ingrained habit for many to not interrupt unnecessarily.

Hiring family is another example of a cultural difference among our JBKnowledge offices. Nepotism is when you hire a family member or very close friend into a position where you could potentially influence that position. It's not common to hire family in the U.S. unless the business is family owned. It can be a challenging environment. In Argentina, our first hire was Sebastian's dad. He had been a business owner and exited his business, so he was available and wanted something to do. He knew every local contact we needed. In the U.S., this may have been a red flag because he was reporting directly to his son. But Argentines believe strongly that when you have people with integrity, it's a no-brainer.

In Argentina, we now have roughly fifteen employees related to someone in the company. We made sure to separate them into different chains of command and have checks and balances in place, but I now love hiring family members in Argentina. This may seem like a small change in my thinking, but I had to suspend a lot of rules I'd held tightly since a young age. Remember, although my dad took me to the office every week for years, he wouldn't even hire *me* at his company!

Argentina also taught me how imperative it is to get to know your people. With my U.S. employees, none of us had the same childhood or upbringing. With my Argentine employees, none of us had even *similar* childhoods or upbringings. A person's motivations are intrinsically tied to their family, culture, and childhood experiences. When you don't share any of those, it is a completely different ballgame when building a relationship with and motivating them.

Americans are very portable. When I built a business here in the United States, people worked from all over. They don't always place value in being in the same town as their family. The exact opposite is true in Argentina. The vast majority of my staff puts a very high value on being at their grandmother's house every Sunday. In Argentina, we learned it was too hard to recruit somebody from another town to move. To expand our employee hiring base, we had to open another office in another town.

We also learned very quickly that if an important soccer game was on in Argentina, it's best to accommodate rather than fight it. Giving employees the means (and beverages) to watch a match at the office increased morale way more than making them lie about why they were calling in sick. I'll never forget one of our U.S. employees telling me that while she was working from our Argentina office, she went to a hospital for blood work during a World Cup match. They told her, "Sorry, you'll have to wait until after the game," because all the doctors and technicians were in the waiting room watching the match with the patients. You can't fight culture, and in so many cases, it's more fun not to.

At first, it was hard for me to make accommodations for things that we would never do in the U.S. until I realized our U.S. employees got other perks that didn't exist in Argentina. This comparison game can be exhausting, but it also spurred us to share experiences and opportunities across continents. For example, when we realized our U.S. employees could take advantage of a local gym membership, Sebastian and I made a personal investment to open a gym near our office in Salta so employees could work out there for free. There are no simple solutions. It takes time, understanding, and many conversations to understand what people of different cultures truly value.

During our growth phase, we continued to expand our presence. We added a second office in Argentina to hire more developers and designers. We expanded to a suburb of Cape Town, South Africa, to spread our support team across more time zones for customer service. We believe the future of business is global. We believe you can't be in the technology business and not think and sell and source globally. Our economies are simply too integrated at this point, and you lose a significant competitive advantage in the technology business if you don't have a global supply chain, a global customer base, and a global support system. We focus on delivering our products and operating our company in multiple languages, geographies, time zones, and currencies.

This requires us to understand exchange rates, political climates, and foreign laws and have legal and accounting vendors that can help us do that. We want to continue to build and sell products internationally, and we want to continue to operate all over the world. As a bootstrapped company, operating internationally was a huge factor in our success. Not just because of the competitive costs, but because of the talent and culture those offices have added to our team.

Restructuring and Tightening the Belt

In 2012, we realized if we ever wanted to sell off a product and keep our core business, we had to separate our product and service entities. This would make a sale easier in so many ways. We'd have dedicated financial statements, tax returns, and client service agreements. It would also allow us to protect the intellectual property and revenue of each of our offerings by isolating them. We split JBKnowledge into three legal entities: JBKnowledge, our software-development services and consulting company; SmartBid, our construction-bid software product; and SmartCompliance, a certificate-of-insurance–tracking software product we'd started building for the insurance industry. While we patted ourselves on the back for the strategic decision, seeing the entities separately showed us how poorly we'd been tracking our budgets and resources.

It took us almost a year to fully adopt a budget template, process, and tracking system for each department in each entity. Once the numbers were in front of us, we could clearly see we weren't netting what we should have been. The business had grown enough that the small expenses had compounded and turned big. We had gotten lazy, financially, because we weren't struggling to make ends meet anymore; we were also excited about what we were building and had hired a ton of people.

As our business was growing, its cash requirements accelerated. We always set a target of having two months' operating cash in the bank, and when our business doubled in size every year, so did our requirement for cash reserves. The only way to build those cash reserves was by generating a profit and leaving it in the business. So, in order to maintain our cash reserve as we grew, we had to spend less than we made. When we restructured into three companies, we saw more clearly which entities had the most revenue, which had the most expenses, and which were eating up all our cash. It was time to tighten the belt.

Sometimes, no matter how long you've been in business, you have to tighten your belt, especially while scaling.

"Short-term sacrifice, long-term gain" is not just a boot-strapping philosophy; it's a mathematical formula. Despite what growth hackers may claim, you don't solve losses with scale. You only scale the losses. Remember, growth isn't the only metric that matters, especially if you want to have some money for yourself after an exit. If your unit economics suck, they're going to keep sucking.

I remember a client we worked with in the early 2000s who didn't value leaving capital in the business. Every year, they took out all the profit made and zeroed out the bank account. In their minds, they made the money, so it was theirs. This perspective is not wrong, but it lacks foresight. I remember the owner told me they spent over $40,000 on a new swimming pool for their house. Why did I care? Because when it came time to pay our invoices, they asked for extensions because they said they had a cash crunch. I got very upset because I knew where my money was—in the brick and stucco of that pool behind the owner's house. The executives there were scrambling to find additional funding before they couldn't delay the bills any longer, and the business had to shut down. Luckily, I had reinvested my profit, and I had cash reserves to pay my team while I waited for their payment.

The best budgeting advice my dad gave me in the years after 2012 was to cut our expected revenue by half and double our expected expenses. As entrepreneurs, it's our job to be optimistic about what we're building and launching—but it's our duty to be conservative when crunching the numbers. The unfortunate reality is that too many things can happen that will reduce your revenue. This lesson hit companies really hard during the COVID-19 pandemic lockdowns of

2020. Organizations with no cash reserves went out of business quickly or were barely saved by government bailouts. During our painful growth years, we learned to build a budget based on historical data, sales projections, and assuming everything can go wrong.

The most effective, and least painful, ways we learned to quickly tighten the belt and prioritize cash on hand were based on one unshakeable commitment Sebastian and I made to each other: do whatever is necessary to not lay off staff. We loved our people, and people are so expensive to hire and train that it's highly counterproductive to lose them.

That doesn't mean it wasn't painful or there weren't staff who quit anyway. Our primary measures for cutting back expenses often seemed drastic and unfair. We closed any open job postings. We did not replace any staff that left. We canceled software licenses that weren't critical. We cut discretionary spending—meals, entertainment, travel, office snacks, etc. We cut ad budgets that couldn't directly point to return on investment (ROI). If it came to it, Sebastian and I cut our own pay so we never had to cut our employees' pay. Along with immediate changes to cut expenses, we had other measures in place to allow for quick adjustments. For example, we learned to keep our leases short. I've learned landlords hate turnover, especially if you pick a small town like we did, and they'll have no problem renewing and renegotiating your lease year after year. You don't have to commit yourself to a massive ten-year expense in an unpredictable startup environment. Especially if you're in the tech industry and working from home is always an option, make sure your office lease isn't what makes you go bankrupt. I've seen too many startups waste money on ego-driven expenses like fancy offices.

Another philosophy we learned to live by was to try not to have a single client that was bigger than our profit margin. That way, if any client left, we could still break even until we replaced them. While big clients are exciting and valuable, you never want the loss of one to eliminate your profitability. Financial management is a beast, and there are many ways to approach it, but I found that succinct principles like this were the easiest for our team to understand and internalize. As my father and Dave Ramsey say, "If your outgo exceeds your income, your upkeep is your downfall."

Pricing Your Products

During SmartBid's high-growth phase from 2010 to 2017, our expenses were climbing but so was demand for our product, so we had multiple opportunities to review our pricing strategy.

When he had his Teflon business, my dad would always say, "Don't nickel and dime people, take care of your clients." His clients would call in needing a very small part and asking how much it would cost. Dad typically said, "Don't worry about it. We'll just send it to you." These little parts would get sent out, no questions asked. They only cost a few bucks, but that gesture was worth a whole lot more. It endeared the client to my dad's company because they knew that if they spent most of their budget with my dad, they didn't have to worry about little inconveniences here and there. As those clients increased their spending with my dad, it more than paid for the small parts shipped.

When you sell time, like we do in our services division, you have to pay close attention to how your client views you. They shouldn't be viewing you as an attorney. You don't want clients worried about calling you and wondering if you're tracking the minutes as they go by. You want to show them you're focused on their problem, not the invoice. Ironically, this tends to make them value you more and be even more willing to pay the invoice for your time.

When you sell a product for a set advertised price though, there are so many more factors to consider. The first thing I did when setting the price for SmartBid was to ask every prospect I could what they were paying currently for their construction-bidding solutions. Whether their solution was a dedicated software, an intern doing it manually, or a hodge-podge of Excel and email, I wanted to understand what they were paying. This seems common sense, but I encounter a lot of salespeople who are afraid to ask prospects what they pay competitors. Remember, in business-to-business (B2B) tech, it's not a personal expense, and most professionals are happy to tell you what they use and what their company pays for them to use it. Your prospects are your best source of intelligence when setting pricing—especially when they don't become clients, as they are often willing to tell you exactly what your product lacked in pricing or features. So we set pricing for SmartBid based on prospect discussions and some financial analysis and began selling.

In 2015, multiple VC-funded competitors came onto the market offering their construction-bid software free, or "freemium" as we like to call it in SaaS. "Freemium" means it appears free, but the free version usually only gets you limited functionality with a hard sales pitch to upgrade to get the functionality you really need. Those competitors were ignoring pricing to focus on market share. They were ignoring the forest for the trees. I've only seen this work for the truly remarkable, disruptive, non-replicable products that are so revolutionary that an exit before profitability is possible. Very few companies can pull that off, and almost no bootstrapped companies can.

So, we had a big decision to make. We could have developed a freemium version of SmartBid, but we didn't have, nor did we want, the investor funding that would have been required to stay in business. Instead, we revisited our values as a company and raised our entry-level price point by 20 percent. We decided we wanted to compete on the quality and value of our software product and get the right customers who understood that. We justified our pricing through customer service agents who always picked up the phone, regular product updates, and a personalized focus on every request our users submitted. They weren't getting the same responsiveness or attention to detail from the freemium competitors.

A bootstrapped company has to price its products so that it makes money fairly soon. This can be hard when competing with funded companies. A bootstrapped company has to study consumer psychology, industry trends, and economics. To set pricing to reach profitability, it has to carefully evaluate the value its product brings to the buyer and where that buyer will get the budget from. Are you selling to a cost center (like IT) or a revenue center (like sales)? Does your product prevent future costs or save costs now? Or the trickiest category, does your product just provide entertainment? Finally, should people pay per unit, per user, or by activity?

In the construction software industry, we saw Procore come in and break the mold by doing a usage-based pricing model. Buyers complained at first; they wanted per-user pricing, but the usage-based pricing slowly began to make sense, and now, it's what I encourage most SaaS founders to explore. Usage-based pricing can be tied directly to business activity and results; it's more quantifiable and reportable than tying your product's value to various users. The other big problem with user-based pricing is that it's hard to enforce due to user account sharing.

There is no formula to determine your product pricing, only questions you'll have to do your best to answer based on your values. Then, go test your answers.

Fixating on Competitors

When a football team gets ready for a game, they get ready to compete against a specific team. They fixate on that opponent—their plays, their players. They learn how to strategize against their opponent's specific strengths and weaknesses. They watch endless amounts of game film.

While this works for many sports teams, it doesn't work for tech companies. The purpose of our game, or business, isn't to beat our competitor at feature development; it's to win over as many clients as possible. This would be like if football games' sole objective was to see which team could get the biggest crowd to cheer the loudest.

You can't treat a startup like a football team. You have to fixate on the problem, not the competitor. In the early days of scaling our SmartBid bidding software clients in the construction market, I fixated on a competitor. I'm a competitive person, and it fueled my work. It also led to dissatisfaction in the areas I knew we just couldn't compete on—like funding. I eventually learned that developing an amicable business relationship with this competitor would help me learn what I needed to know about them to position us against them. You know what they say, keep enemies close but your SaaS competitors closer.

We got to the point with this competitor where we'd call each other if our sales guys were misbehaving—using aggressive sales tactics or outdated feature comparisons. We built a mutual respect that kept communication open. This relationship also led to them eventually acquiring our product—but we'll get to that later.

One day in 2015, we received a form submission on the SmartBid website requesting a demo. This happened multiple times a day. As usual, the lead went into our customer relationship management (CRM) system and pinged our lead generation team. They'd call to qualify the prospect and schedule a demo with our sales team if it made sense. Turns out, this particular lead was a secret shopper.

We had competitors' employees request demos previously under personal emails and false names, but we hadn't had someone put this much time into it. They built a website for this fake construction company—it had phone numbers that worked and a purchased domain name with dedicated email addresses. The fake company even had a social media presence! Whoever orchestrated it should probably start a marketing agency for how quickly they ramped that all up.

They went to market with this fake company and requested demos from not only us but other competitors in the industry. I discovered it by comparing notes with competitors we were friendly with, and we found that this same company name existed in all our CRM databases. When I confronted the CEO of that competitor about their fake construction company, they said, "Oh, that's our secret-shopper program." As if it was normal and acceptable.

You can have secret-shopper programs in the retail, residential, and dining industries, but when you're tying up a salesperson's time and viewing and recording proprietary software information, that enters the world of corporate espionage. In my mind, this behavior was highly unethical and, in some states, illegal. I was livid.

Then came another competitor. They had come onto the scene as the new hotness. I'm not going to lie—they had us all worried, especially me. They had a beautiful user interface that looked like all the latest apps you use today, and they were price-cutting the rest of us like crazy by subsidizing their money with venture capital funds. They were formidable, until they started taking on investor money.

After their first round of funding, the unethical, grow-at-all-costs behavior began—which included secret shopping and recording competitor demos. We heard murmurs from other competitors and even received emails from our clients, saying, "Who are these guys? Check out this email." The emails were aggressive, included completely falsified numbers on products like ours, included screenshots from their secret-shopper demos, and all but shamed our clients into taking their call. I'm not going to say it didn't amuse me that our clients just forwarded those emails to me and said, "Get a load of this."

I could go on, but the reason I'm sharing this story is that I can now admit I gave way too much energy to both of those competitors. I fixated. It wasn't until I realized they were their own worst enemies that I remembered to focus on what I was building. I was grateful for the kick in the butt they gave us to improve our messaging and UX/UI (it inspired us to establish an entire team around this!) and for the lesson in how not to take on funding partners.

Fixating on competitors prevents you from focusing on your team and customers. If you survive long enough, you'll see many competitors come and go. If you spend too much time watching competitors, you'll lose sight of your customers and what they need from you. You'll especially miss what *no one* is doing *yet* by assuming your competitor knows exactly what clients need. That's a big assumption that limits your innovation and puts you in a reactionary seat.

Scaling Requires Systems

In bootstrapping, you focus so much on testing and pivoting to achieve cash flow that process can go out the window. This is fine when you're a team of five to ten and everyone is brought in at the same level and motivated similarly. As you scale, that dynamic changes dramatically. Each new employee, product, or service adds exponentially more complexity and need for communication. If systems aren't in place before you scale, you'll break before you realize how bad you need them. If those systems aren't based on shared values, you'll never build a culture that scales.

As a company, we hit a breaking point in 2016. We'd scaled too quickly. I had also scaled personally as I became a city councilman in College Station. I'd always wanted to serve in local politics and give back to the city that'd become my home and the home of our company. I thought the timing worked out because we were hiring people to handle more internally. *I can delegate more,* I thought. *This is a good time to finally pursue politics.*

What I didn't foresee was that hiring was just the beginning—we needed all hands on deck to train, mentor, and learn from our new hires and make sure everyone was in the right role. And as the founder, I was the one with the crazy vision, and no one could sell it like I could. I expected every other executive and manager to have the same motivation and vision as me—but how could they? Their entire career and personal wealth wasn't tied into this company. They had hobbies and families and other things on their minds. I quickly realized that until we hit a significant level of profitability, I had two choices. I'd always have to be on deck *or* I'd have to create way more clarity and delegate way more authority. I was always going to be our biggest hitter unless I gave others the same incentive, motivation, and authority I had. Since I wasn't taking on investors or equity partners, I had to really think about how to do that.

Ken Dewitt entered my life like a genie from a lamp. Ken was a Certified Public Accountant (CPA) for construction companies when I met him, but he told me he was pivoting away from being a CPA. His dad had worked himself to death by a heart attack at a young age. After witnessing this, Ken said, "Nope, I will not be Hurricane Ken (a nickname from his employees at the time) anymore," and sought a different path. He looked for a system that could bring balance, accountability, and health to his organization. When he found it, he decided he wanted to help other companies and entrepreneurs learn it. He had read a book called *Traction* by Gino Wickman and was training to be one of the first Entrepreneurial Operating System (EOS) implementers based on that methodology. After we met, I subscribed to his newsletter and proceeded to receive, in my inbox, all the rhetorical questions that made him sound like a psychic. *Is your team feeling burnt out? Are you struggling to pivot but also stay on track toward goals? Are you struggling with being the visionary and trying to operate at scale? Does your team get to make strategic decisions, or do you hold them tightly? Are you hitting the ceiling in growth? Do you have documented processes? If not, why not?*

His insights and email marketing strategy worked brilliantly on me, and Ken became *our* implementer for the EOS. My staff more lovingly refers to him, though, as our Business Therapist. The first time he traveled to meet with us, he said, "I'm going to present to your team on the first night; if you don't like what you hear, you owe me nothing, and I'll head home in the morning." It's now six years later, and we really just wish he'd move into our office and live there permanently. I always say you need to have a really good accountant, banker, and attorney. Now I'd say that a really good EOS implementer is just as essential.

There are amazing books out there on EOS. Start with *Traction* by Gino Wickman and supporting books like *What the Heck is EOS?* Then read *Good to Great* and *Great by Choice* by Jim Collins. I'm not going to teach you EOS. I am going to emphasize how it changed my life and how our company would have been transformed so much earlier had we done something, anything, like it earlier.

So it's 2016, and we are hitting a ceiling as a company. As we grew, I had delegated responsibilities but not authority. We had too many efforts going, too many shared teams and budgets, and not enough focus. Sebastian and I had somewhat split the company in half, each managing the departments we felt best suited to manage. We kept wondering why we got so frustrated with each other. Our teams were frustrated too. There wasn't a clear vision, operating system, or decision-making apparatus. The disarray was palpable.

We had values that we believed in and worked by, but we had never written them down, so when we began to implement EOS with Ken, we started there. We met as a leadership team and described our favorite employees. We quickly found they had similar traits and values that resonated with the leadership team. From that list of employees and traits, for the first time, we agreed on and wrote down our core values as a company, and we wrote them in order of importance.

After we documented our values for the first time, we committed to sharing them with the team through every medium possible. We put them on the walls of our offices, worked them into our employee reviews, and used them in every hiring interview.

JBKnowledge
Core Values:

1. Do the right thing—even when no one is looking. Exhibit integrity and honesty in all you do.

2. Be self-motivated and resourceful. Have a positive attitude; do the best you can with what you have.

3. Show respect to everyone—be a JBK ambassador 24/7. Teammates, clients, vendors, and others deserve to be treated fairly and professionally.

4. Think Lean. Improve efficiency and eliminate waste.

5. Have each other's backs. We are a team—here to educate, support, and help each other grow.

6. Enjoy the ride and geek out. Love your work, love your teammates, and let us help you find that inner nerd.

Next, we agreed we needed a documented vision built on those values to guide the company into the future and inspire the day-to-day. We built one-, three-, and ten-year vision statements with qualitative and quantitative metrics to help us measure how we get there.

Lastly, we put systems in place that were simple, repeatable, and non-negotiable. We changed our meeting structures and agendas. We customized our project management system—an internal product called SmartEnterprise—around our quarterly planning and weekly meetings. We committed to going all in and seeing where we ended up.

How did it go? Well, the best example I can give you is from March 2020. When the world went into lockdown, we didn't panic. We didn't even need to schedule emergency meetings. Our regular meeting structure and cadence gave employees the support and discussion they needed to adapt, and our system was 100 percent executable from home. We talked about physical and mental health more often in those meetings, but the system supported everyone through a difficult time without requiring big changes.

Systems need infrastructure, not just people and processes, but tools. SmartEnterprise was the first software product we built at JBKnowledge in our early years. I built the first version in my dorm room. I mapped it out within a month of starting the business. We needed a small-business enterprise resource planning (ERP) system for project management and accounting. We still use it to run our whole company, and it's been a labor of love, hate, and sweat.

When we finally implemented EOS, we realized we should take SmartEnterprise seriously as the infrastructure for that system. We dedicated time and teams to this internal software system, which allowed us to practice solving problems and using the software we developed. As a technology company, it also helped us to eat our own dog food. If we won't use our software that we write, who are we to build it for clients? And let me tell you, our employees have been formidable SmartEnterprise clients over the years. That's when you really test your mettle, writing code that you and your team have to use daily.

People, values, vision, systems, tools—we looked at these in an entirely new way after 2016. There isn't a single person on our leadership team who wouldn't agree that it was one of the most pivotal years of our company. EOS changed our lives and the course of our company.

CHAPTER **8**

INNOVATION DOESN'T HAPPEN IN SPARE TIME

As we entered the growth years at JBKnowledge, we were focused on making our team healthy, our products profitable, and our systems scalable. It would have been easy at this stage to focus on what was working and quit pushing the envelope to explore new tech and product offerings. That's what a good bootstrapper would do, right? Not in this book. The moment you stop pushing your vision and team to think about what comes next is the moment you start the timer to your company becoming obsolete. You become a sitting duck just waiting on disruption.

In the startup industry, we love to use the word "disruption," but we don't talk about what it really means. A friend of mine, Brett Young, defines disruption as a business-model change where segments of an industry cannot adapt. We don't listen to cassette tapes anymore, but the music industry is still around. I recently visited my parents' house and found all the photos they have of my childhood—roughly two hundred photos from 1979 to 1999. I have two daughters and roughly two hundred photos of them from a camping trip we took one weekend. We don't develop much film anymore, but we definitely take more pictures than ever.

So, industries persist, but companies get disrupted. They get disrupted because of a decision made to stop innovating long before the disruption happens. I've encountered many CEOs, some even speakers on innovation, who talk a big game about disruption and innovation, but when you ask their employees how they're experimenting, they'll list all the things they can't get approved. The only thing innovative about many companies is that they say they're innovative.

So how do you actually be innovative? What does that even mean? We learned it's using people, processes, and technology to advance your company and get ahead of the pack. Innovating means setting a new pace for those around you and, at the same time, fixing what bugs you to eliminate waste. Those who are really great at innovating are the mad scientists of our generation.

What comes to mind when I say "mad scientist"? It may be Albert Einstein or it may be Frankenstein. When I think of mad scientists, I think of Lockheed Martin's Skunk Works lab. They are a private entity dedicated to R&D and run by a for-profit organization. They were pivotal in developing planes and drones in the 1960s that would influence space travel. When did you first hear about drones? It wasn't until after 2000 for most people—but Skunk Works was building them forty years before that.

I also think of Google X, "the moonshot factory." Their goal is to impact one hundred million people with every experiment. You may have heard about when they launched balloons over Africa that could last one hundred days at a time and supply WiFi. They attempted to develop contact lenses that can read diabetics' blood-sugar levels. They funded a fascinating project in the built environment for programming buildings. While these efforts may not survive, they demonstrate a willingness to learn and try.

Alexander Graham Bell, Nikola Tesla, Steve Jobs—these mad scientists revolutionized modern society. And they did it with a profit incentive, not just out of sheer nerdiness. They did it in for-profit companies. You're probably thinking how different you are from them and the companies they built—but you're not. You're a mad scientist just for saying, "I want to be an entrepreneur/intrapreneur." You're trying to build profitably, but you're also trying to advance the organization and society. You're not the "Let's see what happens" type—you've proven that by picking up this book. Most likely, you're a tinkerer who loves to build and fix stuff.

Regardless of whether you're an entrepreneur or corporate intrapreneur, you'll learn that the most profitable innovations come from the inside out. Not from watching your competitors or industry to see what happens next, but by pushing your company on the path you believe it should be on next. It's not easy. It's not free. It's not guaranteed success. But when it works, it future-proofs you, as long as you keep on working. Here's what I've learned about innovating through every stage of a company—from startup to multinational corporation—and how we managed to do it while bootstrapping and scaling.

Five Critical Steps of Innovation

So how do you innovate like a mad scientist? How do you build sustainable, competitive advantages that disrupt an industry? How do you develop internal mad scientists who can lead the effort? I would argue that there are five key steps that hold true no matter the revenue, size, or age of your company.

1. Set Audacious Goals

The first component in creating mad scientists is communicating an audacious goal. If your organization does not discuss and set audacious goals, what will your employees reach for? What will you reach for? It's amazing how this works. If the CEO, investors, executives, and innovation

Make innovation a habit and a process.

People, processes, and tools—you need all three to create a culture of innovation, but the most often neglected is process. Every other function of a sustainable business operates on systems and best practices learned from generations of professionals—innovation should be no different.

leaders of the company do not lay out difficult, challenging goals, guess what? They don't happen.

In 1962, President John F. Kennedy told thousands of students at Rice University that the U.S. would go to the moon. "We choose to go to the moon in this decade and do the other things, not because they are easy, but because they are hard." Seven years later, U.S. astronauts landed on the moon, and we did it with less computer processing power than your smartphone has today.

The result of setting audacious goals is not only motivating people to reach them but empowering them to reach them. This starts at the top, and words matter. Words matter in how you communicate the audacious goal but also in how you speak to those who you want to achieve it. I can't tell you how many companies I've spoken to where the founder talks about "Letting those nerdy IT guys do their thing." It's all in good fun (theoretically), but it sends the message that the CEO isn't fully bought in on what they do—this is the opposite of empowering. Empowering means stepping in, learning what your people bring to the table, and inspiring them to contribute in their own way to this audacious goal.

Since I haven't met JFK, I'll give you a more personal anecdote of an audacious goal. There is an electrical subcontractor we worked with based in the Midwest. They are hired by general contractors and owners to install or repair electrical infrastructure in buildings. Like most construction companies, they are in a low-margin business. Unlike most construction companies, the leadership realized this was entirely under their control. The company's typical profit margin on a project was around 8 percent, the industry standard, and they decided to set a goal of doubling that for every project. The company has a productivity tracking and operations team that determined they could achieve this profit margin through a 30x30 rule—thirty feet or thirty seconds. Its construction jobs were taking too long because people and materials were too far apart—tools, trash, bathrooms, etc.—so they adjusted worksite layouts to ensure essential tools and materials were within thirty feet or thirty seconds of where the team was working at any given time. Over eight years, they repeated this mantra and took productivity through the roof. Profitability followed. That boost in cash flowed straight through to the shareholders of the company and to employees in the form of wages. Performance bonuses went up. Everybody in the company won. And they got way more competitive because they were way more productive than their competitors. It was an audacious goal—but only until they got started. Once they achieved their first goal, their CEO set a new and even more audacious goal. They are currently working toward getting all tools and materials within *five* feet or *five* seconds of reach.

An important lesson hidden in this story is that it takes visionaries to craft a goal but operators to execute it. It's important that goals follow George T. Doran's S.M.A.R.T. method and are Specific, Measurable, Attainable, Relevant, and Timely. Had this company not had a productivity team that could identify where and how to increase profit margin, the goal would have just been a pretty slide and talking point, not a workable challenge. Had they not used process and technology, they could not have achieved their goal.

2. Dedicate Staff and Budgets

Every Olympic athlete wants to win Gold, but only a few do what it takes to accomplish it. Your audacious goal needs a dedicated team and budget. And by budget, I don't mean taking an existing budget and adding 5 percent for inflation and a couple new efforts. I mean strategy-based budgeting that involves two short questions that have long answers: What do we want to accomplish? What spending will it take to get there?

It took me longer than I'm proud of to realize that if you want something to have focus and commitment, it needs a dedicated budget and staff. Conflicting priorities create conflicting results. Innovation does not occur in your spare time. People spend their non-working hours with their families and on their hobbies. A bootstrapped entrepreneur may be motivated to innovate in their spare time, but the average employee wants to make an impact during their work hours, and, frankly, that's all you're paying them for. Most companies ask employees to sit in two seats and innovate in their spare time—no wonder it doesn't happen.

Since our first year, we've had innovative developers focused on experimenting and testing new technology at JBKnowledge. The problem was, as we grew, those employees proved so valuable we put them in charge of our most important production and development teams. Eventually, they ran out of time to experiment. When we finally decided to remedy this, we had just over one hundred employees. I told Sebastian, "I want to hire an intern, a computer science major from Texas A&M, and they're going to work directly for me. I'm going to give them desk space, a VR headset, and a 3D printer and see what we can come up with to solve our clients' problems in a new way." As always, Sebastian was on board and helped me figure out how to fund it. I spent about $12,000 on intern labor (because we always pay our interns) and $10,000 on equipment. Within ninety days, he'd developed our first prototype. He then handed that off to our product teams, who developed the first augmented-reality app, called SmartReality, for visualizing construction blueprints. What our team learned from SmartReality pushed an overhaul of our cloud storage and services infrastructure across the company. It also generated some wonderful PR for our other products.

Today, I'm proud to have a dedicated space with whiteboard walls covered in ideas and a dedicated R&D staff who continue to work on true research and development. They have also published research reports from their work that our marketing team loves to use for content and thought leadership. We contribute to open-source code libraries across the internet. We are transforming our business and our industry, and it took dedicated staff and budgets to do it.

3. Define and Prioritize Your Process

Even the most brilliant scientists follow a process. Innovation requires it.

As a die-hard Texas Aggie football fan, it pains me to point to this example, but I must. Let's talk about Nick Saban. Love him or hate him, he's won several NCAA football titles, more than any other coach. He always attributes his success to "the process." How else could a coach turn over his entire coaching and playing staff every four years and keep winning? Because he is maniacal about his process. It is even referred to as "the process." Many books have been written about Saban's process, so I'll leave most of the details to them. But I will say his adherence to a standardized approach to coaching (even down to how long he gives himself to relax after a championship win) has allowed him to deal with incredible turnover and still generate career-defining championship results. Unfortunately, the reality for most of us in business is that we don't operate with a playbook.

Most organizations have a very clear process. I call it SOMP—the "seat of my pants" process. Here's what happens. They wake up, drink their coffee, and commute to work or saunter over to their home office. They open up their computer, check their email, and just start putting out fires. Eight to ten hours later, they've suppressed the fires they could and set reminders to check on the others tomorrow. They're exhausted; they have dinner and wrangle their kids. They fall asleep on the couch or reading a book. They wake up the next day, and they do it all over again. This is life for so many employees and entrepreneurs. It is purely reactive.

This is not how Nick Saban operates. He follows a process that is documented and updated year after year. There's no deviation—it works, and they stick to it.

Our R&D process at JBKnowledge can be best summarized as Discover, Develop, Deploy, Observe, and Respond. We always have a running list of ideas on a giant whiteboard. When we are ready to start a new project, we pick the one that feels right and start the **discovery** process. During the discovery process, we can spend as little as one week before stating, "Nope, let's pick a different project." Other times, we spend twelve to eighteen months studying a problem, talking with potential users, and understanding the market. Until we clearly understand what an MVP should look like and if it is within our capability and desire to build, we do not move on. Next, we **develop** the MVP. This process goes as quickly as possible so we can **deploy** something, a beta version, to get hands on it. The sooner we deploy, the sooner we can **observe** how people use that MVP. With their feedback and our observations, we can **respond** with improvements and ideas or even shut it down to start discovery on something new. If the MVP proves wildly successful, we consider handing it off to our product team immediately to keep building, or we fully dedicate our R&D team to it for a limited amount of time for further testing.

Discovery, Develop, Deploy, Observe, and Respond—whether you use these steps or define your own, it's important you have a documented process and your team knows it by heart.

4. Study the Problem

This has to be repeated. Spend most of your time studying the problem. If you're going to work on solving a problem, follow the saying and spend fifty-five minutes of every hour studying the problem and five minutes designing the solution. Get eyes on the problem from as many angles as possible—get out in the field or walk around the office. In the early days of SmartBid, I sat in cubicles with construction estimators for countless hours, watching them work. It was invaluable. In the tech space, I always say look for highly manual processes involving paper or spreadsheets; these are often low-hanging fruit.

Be aware that innovation and R&D teams are notorious for shiny-object syndrome. They get dedicated teams and budgets and establish amazingly audacious goals. Then, they get fixated on one new hardware or software piece that would make their work look really cool and innovative but isn't necessarily focused on solving any problems. They find an exciting technology, and then they try to find a problem it solves. Mad scientists work to understand an existing (or upcoming) problem completely and think big about the solution. Most importantly, when you solve an existing problem, you have far fewer problems with the next step. You must build things that matter.

5. Focus on Adoption

Step five is to focus on adoption and don't overcomplicate it. Your solutions are only as valuable as they are implementable. Whether it's your R&D team or a commercialization team or other, make sure they are involved early to plan a process to transfer great innovations into the field. This involves a lot more human psychology than most people would like to admit.

I worked with a technologist at a construction company who managed to digitize all the company's jobsite plans and establish virtual design and construction (VDC) stations at the jobsite. This meant touch-screen computers were available to site workers so they could interact with virtual, 3D blueprints whenever they had questions about where this pipe went or how wide this door should be. It was leaps and bounds ahead of most construction sites, which have piles of paper blueprints for workers to sift through, hoping the printouts are the latest ones. Darren Roos, this technologist, was so proud of his accomplishment—until the site workers ignored the stations and continued to request paper printouts. They said they didn't have time to learn the digital navigation. He spent some time brainstorming solutions and ended up at Costco, where he bought a box of king-sized candy bars. He told the crew, "I'm going to hide a Star Wars model of R2D2 in these virtual construction plans every day; the first person to find it every day gets a king-sized candy bar." Within two weeks, 80 percent of the jobsite workers were comfortable using and navigating the virtual plans at the VDC stations. This is gamification at its best.

It wasn't complicated. All it took was a damn candy bar, and he made adoption fun. He learned that people aren't just impressed by cool developments—especially if they don't understand them or know how to use them. Innovators have to be great salespeople too. The sooner you talk about the problem you're studying and the solutions you're building, the sooner people start to get on board and the easier adoption will be at the end. R&D teams shouldn't hide in a cave until they have a revelation. They should be at every client event, every employee social, sharing their progress and building relationships that will establish trust and credibility.

Document and Reflect

After the five critical steps, take the time to document and calculate the ROI. Easier said than done, I know, but if you've spent time studying the problem and can quantify it in hours, dollars, or other metrics, you can quantify it again with your solution and measure the difference. Remember, adoption involves some sales, and you'll want to be able to illustrate why the problem needs fixing and why the customer should adopt your solution to fix it. Once you quantify that difference, or ROI, don't forget to put it in terms that your audience values. If you're talking to the C-suite, it's usually dollars or hours saved. If you're talking to your employees, it's the results they'll see in their pay raises or daily roles.

Most teams wait to do this until the end only to find they have a hard time measuring the "before" and may not have studied the problem well enough. It's like when you renovate your kitchen and forget to take a before photo—how will your social media followers know how well you redesigned? That's why Paul Akers in *2 Second Lean* says to always take a before and after video and share it so everyone can learn from your changes and improvements.

Keep Going

Don't stop tinkering. The result of becoming a mad scientist is understanding how many problems need solutions. You'll start to see them everywhere. Competitive advantages are only sustainable until they're not. Your company will always be looking for the next one, and it can absolutely come from you. Lead the charge of having a "Let's find out" attitude. Naysayers never become innovators. Everyone wants to be a food critic, but only the chefs are remembered. Remember, technology is overwhelming and ever changing, but it's creating a future that is abundant. We live in the most abundant time ever in human history—believe that and start innovating like it.

Corporate Innovators versus Entrepreneurs

One of the great things about being an entrepreneur is you attract and meet more entrepreneurs. Your network becomes an energetic, vibrant mix of visionaries, idealists, and big thinkers. While I owe my fellow entrepreneurs credit for many of my best business decisions, a smaller, less vocal group of innovators have driven so much of my company's success. These innovators don't run their own companies, they aren't always in the C-suite, and they don't claim the title entrepreneur—though they should. These innovators operate within corporate structures built decades, or even centuries, before they were hired. They look at inefficiency, friction, and industry problems, and instead of saying, "I'm going to go build a company that fixes this," they stick around and say, "How can our company fix this?"

Corporate intrapreneurs, or corporate innovators, as I like to call them, are a different breed of professional. Like entrepreneurs, they're undaunted by failure and naysayers, and they're driven by a passion that goes beyond paychecks. Like entrepreneurs, they're bootstrapping and trying to make big things happen on a small or non-existent budget. Like entrepreneurs, they're selling a vision of something maybe only they can see.

I couldn't write a book on bootstrapping, entrepreneurism, and innovation without acknowledging the contributions of corporate innovators who have influenced how I think about all three of those concepts. While corporate innovators usually have a guaranteed paycheck, I'd argue that's one of the *only* things that separates them from entrepreneurs. Both parties can learn so much from each other, and both parties need each other. As startups grow and scale, they need to keep big thinkers and innovative talent, not run them off to start their own competitive companies.

My company has worked hard to support and connect with corporate innovators over the years—they're often our most powerful advocates and clients. I told a few of them about this book and what I'm trying to accomplish, and they agreed to share their perspectives on their work, innovation, and how they're building a future for more mad scientists like them.

The Resume of a Corporate Innovator

Like entrepreneurs, corporate innovators don't fit in a box. They come from all backgrounds, all departments, and all skillsets. Chris Griffith, now CIO and COO at UPC Insurance, was developing technology during the dot-com boom of the 2000s before he found his way into the insurance industry. "I was working with startups that all failed during the dot-com boom. One was developing a business-to-consumer (B2C) platform for furniture sales—like so many tech failures in that decade, it was before smartphones and before its time. But I learned a ton about rapid software development that I soon discovered the insurance industry needed desperately."

Travis Voss, Leader of Innovation Technology at Helm Mechanical, a construction services company, had never worked in the construction industry until five years ago. "I drove by this office for the first forty years of my life and had no idea what the company did." Voss started developing software in the 1990s; he was self-taught. When Helm began exploring VDC software and services to better support their construction projects, they sought a technologist who geeked out on software and was willing to learn the construction industry. Voss was recommended by a friend for the job.

Rob Galbraith, Founder and CEO of Forestview Insights and author of *The End of Insurance As We Know It*, had no intention of working in the insurance industry either. As an economics major whose first job was at the Federal Reserve, he found his way to insurance via the financial-services sector. He grew to appreciate the impact of insurance when catastrophes hit. When he became the Director of Underwriting Research at USAA, his ability to improve catastrophe-claims processing and work with startups across the industry to do so solidified his resume as a corporate innovator.

Rick Khan, Chief Innovation Officer at STO Building Group, spent sixteen years at Mortenson Construction, one of the first in the building industry to fully embrace the technology revolution that VDC would bring about. To learn the emerging technologies he didn't understand yet, he collaborated with university researchers and startups to figure out how to pilot projects together that would help solve his construction company's (and the industry's) challenges. He helped build the model of innovation and R&D that construction companies around the world are now trying to deploy.

If you ask these professionals what it means to be a corporate innovator and if they consider themselves as such, they answer humbly but confidently. "The most important trait is that they don't fear failure. They see it as a necessary step in the process and not a destination," answered Griffith. When asked if this can be developed, he noted it takes more than just the "Maverick" personality (if you're familiar with the Predictive Index behavioral assessment) to achieve innovation. If failure is scary for you, find a Maverick to partner with because they'll need someone with a fear of failure to lead execution and operations within reasonable parameters. Voss described a corporate innovator, and himself, as "someone who treats their position as if it's its own small business within the company. My customers are the employees within the company. I'm selling myself as a service to the rest of the company." He noted more people should consider corporate innovation—it's an opportunity to explore the entrepreneurial mindset with a guaranteed paycheck to fall back on.

Defining Corporate Innovation

If you ask those four professionals how their companies approach innovation, you'll get varied approaches to a similar mindset. For Khan, his innovation efforts are focused on helping people understand the key business problems his company faces (internally or externally), who is impacted by those problems, and how to harness his team's expertise to prioritize and solve those problems. He cited a *Harvard Business Review* article from 2012 titled "Managing Your Innovation Portfolio" in which the authors, Bansi Nagji and Geoff Tuff, argue that innovation covers three key areas. Seventy percent of organizational efforts toward innovation should be incremental and focused on process improvements and, in lean terminology, "fixing the process problems your people face." Twenty percent of innovation efforts should look at what adjacent industries are deploying successfully and how that innovation can be adapted for your company. The final 10 percent of innovation focus and budget is transformational innovation—the big new ideas, business models, and technologies that sound and look sexy. Khan's point in citing this article is that companies often think "innovation" is only that 10 percent category, and this prevents companies from risking time and money to pursue it because it's the hardest category to find success in—when, in fact, you can justify (and produce return on) 90 percent of your innovation budget through process improvements and adjacency and only focus 10 percent of that budget on the transformational, bold initiatives and hypotheses. Galbraith added to this concept by noting, "Innovation should be both offensive (keeping up with competition) and defensive (swinging for the fence)." In addition, success in defensive innovation should help fund the offensive innovation efforts.

Galbraith also believes innovation needs to be both a culture and a discipline. While the startup world has driven powerful rhetoric (and evidence) of the *culture* of innovation, the *discipline* of innovation is less understood. Think about HR, product development, sales, and even marketing. These departments follow standard processes, procedures, and best practices shared across industries. SEO is a discipline studied by content marketers. Cold calling is a discipline studied by outbound sales managers. What are corporate innovators studying? Are the disciplines documented, shared, and improved by each new innovation department that "figures it out"? Galbraith argues that no, the discipline of innovation is not well documented or shared.

Where should the discipline of innovation start? We often

think of the ambitious individual with an idea and a pitch to take to leadership. The popular narrative around innovation headlines the underdog, a bottom-up approach. All four of those corporate innovators agree that's not enough. The only way they've seen corporate innovation be successful is with a top-down approach—even if it means getting *just one* C-suite executive on board.

The Process of Corporate Innovation

To share and build the discipline of innovation, I asked my friends how their company structures, staffs, and budgets for innovation. Voss is a great example to start with, as he's the only employee with "innovation" in his title at the moment and a department of one. He serves as an internal consultant to all departments—whether they want to implement a new process or technology. He has the authority to review and prioritize their challenges and request budgets from his boss, the VP of Operations, to help solve them. He also sees a big part of his role as helping with adoption and implementation to ensure their innovation efforts don't result in a buildup of unused tools. To grow the department, he hopes someday to hire more strategic consultants like him, business analysts to conduct user interviews to help diagnose and detail the problems that need solving, coders who can connect applications or solve smaller challenges with simple scripts, and finally, support staff to help their company's overloaded IT team with application and user support. Over the years, Voss has noticed his innovation efforts featured more and more in the company's business-development efforts and sees this as a strong signal that growth of his department is inevitable.

As a C-suite executive, Khan has the authority and budget to structure a larger innovation effort and team. They've built Centers for Excellence and Innovation (CEI) embedded within each division of the company. Participating individuals help identify challenges and ideas their departments face that could impact other divisions and the profitability of the company. The Innovation Executive Committee, led by Khan, identifies common denominators and projects with far-reaching impacts and builds cross-functional teams to address them. While Khan has dedicated budget and staff for innovation projects, he notes, "Innovation teams get too cocky about what they can do themselves." Some of his most successful (and profitable) efforts over the years were due to finding external university and startup partners to help solve problems. His current role has even evolved into managing an investment strategy for STO Building Group, where he gathers angel investors from across the architecture, engineering, and construction (AEC) industry to fund startups they all can benefit from working with.

On his latest innovation project, Griffith, as COO, sent an email to the entire company, explaining the new product they would develop and asking who wanted to be involved. He made sure managers understood the value of the product to the company and employees knew this wouldn't change their pay or title immediately. He received over fifty responses and little pushback from their managers, who figured out how to let them dedicate X hours a week to the innovation project. Those who participated received company-wide recognition, and some now work on the new product team as it scales into its own business. Griffith noted that, especially at large, traditional corporate businesses, many employees crave a new opportunity. Innovation projects can provide that so those employees don't jump ship to go work for a startup. He also noted that the key to their success in innovation projects is to build the prototype, then pass it on to the more experienced teams to build a sustainable business. Innovation teams should be experts at rapid problem solving and development on a budget, and they can't confuse that with being experts at scaling a sustainable business.

All of these innovators agreed that innovation efforts and teams should follow a discipline and process, but they should have slightly different metrics than other teams at your company. The metrics they measure success by should include figuring out what *won't* work. To summarize, their success has to include a metric for learning and for failure. Khan would often start an innovation project pitch by making sure the leadership team knew that success meant *completing* a proof of concept, NOT profitability in launching a new product or other result. This is why a top-down approach is critical because leadership has to understand and approve of this mentality from the beginning. That doesn't mean innovation teams get a blank check, though, Galbraith clarified. It means their metrics and efforts should be incremental. They should be allotted a pot of money with room for failure but should still be expected to replenish that pot to a certain percentage before receiving additional approvals.

Success and Failure—It's All the Same

I asked these corporate innovators about a project they're really proud of—whether it was a raging success or whether they failed spectacularly and learned a lifetime's worth of lessons from it. The answers were mixed and "to be determined."

While at Mortenson, Khan noticed their solar business was exploding, and the biggest inefficiency on those construction projects was the breadth of the construction sites (think miles and miles of solar farmland) and having to move equipment daily to the next production site. He wondered how robotics could help move trucks, materials, and equipment autonomously overnight so everything was ready when workers arrived each morning. He approached a startup called Built Robotics, which helped develop a pilot—an autonomous skid steer that could move large pallets overnight. While the pilot was very successful, Built Robotics wasn't willing to scale the effort nationally because it wasn't part of the company's roadmap and didn't align with their business objectives. Khan learned a valuable lesson in partnerships and understanding what would make a pilot successful not just for his company but the partner company as well.

Griffith's team recently built his company's first direct-to-consumer insurance platform, Skyway.com, in nine months. It started as an idea from the CEO, and over nine months, it evolved into a volunteer force of employees across the company, a dedicated technology development team, and some help from our JBKnowledge R&D team. It is now UPC's newest business line. At the completion of development, Griffith's team handed the product off to their experienced product management teams to launch and scale. "The success of this project is that our direct-to-consumer platform now exists. The demand isn't quite there yet, but it will be. And we'll be ahead of the competition."

"My favorite innovation story isn't that sexy, but it was impactful," Voss shared. When he first started working for Helm, and the construction industry, he noticed the company hired a local contractor to perform laser scanning about once a month. By laser scanning existing construction sites, Voss' teams could get a better idea of the structures and foundations they would be renovating or rebuilding in order to build better material estimates and project plans. They paid the contractor roughly $25,000 a year for laser-scanning services. Voss got curious and asked a local vendor how much it would cost to buy a laser scanner—the answer was $65,000. He asked the laser-scanner vendor if they would loan him one of their devices for a week. They agreed. He performed scans for a week to show the team the value of having a scanner on hand. Within that week, he easily made the case to purchase the company's first scanner of its own.

Galbraith's insurance-carrier employer realized it needed a digital offering for small and mid-sized businesses (SMBs) because its brick-and-mortar insurance brokers pursued larger companies (and commissions) and didn't spend their time going door to door for SMBs. Competitors would scoop up these SMBs instead, and his company would miss out as those SMBs scaled into much bigger companies. However, they didn't want to build a direct-to-consumer model that cut the brokers out and incentivized them going to work for other carriers. Galbraith went to his IT department, and they said they were swamped and couldn't help. So, he found a startup building a similar product to what he envisioned, and he built a mutually beneficial pilot plan and budget. Together, they built a digital platform that their brokers could white label and use to bring on more SMBs digitally with the same commission structure they had for in-person sales. Though the pilot was a success, after the launch, Galbraith learned the tough lesson that they didn't have an experienced product manager to own and scale the product. As a result, the product hasn't scaled and seen adoption as quickly as it could have.

The Next Generation

If you haven't noticed a theme already, innovation involves defining and sharing success. It's about getting leadership bought in and getting employees excited to contribute. How are these corporate innovators doing that? How are they cultivating more innovators at their companies and in their networks?

Galbraith emphasized that innovation cannot be a segmented approach handed off over the fence. If you're solving a problem for a set of employees or clients, tell them about it from the beginning. Get them involved. Only then can you truly study the problem and share the lessons or success.

Khan can tell you that marketing and innovation go hand in hand. His teams have seen success because he's learned how to tell their story across the company. With each innovation project, success or failure, they produce videos and recaps of what they've learned that are shared company-wide. Individuals contributing to innovation are recognized at all levels and championed.

Griffith continues to give the entire company opportunities to work on innovation projects by sending out notices of new projects and the skill sets needed. He's made joining the innovation efforts as easy as replying to an email and saying, "Here's how I want to help."

As a one-man team, Voss takes a hands-on approach to developing more innovators and offers to spend time with new interns, jobsite superintendents, and anyone else touching technology daily. He stays up to date on their workflows and makes sure they know who he is, what he does, and how to contact him if they have a need or an idea.

I'm excited about the next generation of entrepreneurs and corporate innovators—and not just because the four innovation leaders I've highlighted above are helping develop them. I'm excited because they'll have more documentation, examples, and mentors to study. They'll have more data than ever to make the case for innovation. And they'll be able to apply decades of successful bootstrapping lessons to their efforts.

Become Your Own PR

While my team geeked out every day on what we were working on at JBKnowledge, it was hard to get the media to do so. Whether we didn't have the size, contacts, or industry sex appeal, we just weren't able to get coverage on the products, vision, and experiments we were running. We wanted people to know how we were pushing the industry forward so they could jump on board.

There's a reason PR firms are so expensive. PR is hard, and despite the volume of publications out there, there is still limited airtime. We spent money on PR firms and just weren't seeing progress. We couldn't find events that were worth the booth and travel costs. We didn't have a lot of cash, but we had smart people, and we had time. So finally, I said out loud, "Why can't we experiment with becoming our own PR?"

This is a slippery slope in bootstrapping. It's easy to say, "Let's do X ourselves," and have "X" turn into "everything." Next thing you know, your team is completely burnt out and you've built a Frankenstein process of operations that doesn't scale. But there are opportunities to DIY if you 1) have a passion for it and 2) commit to making it a priority and not just a cost savings.

In 2012, I had really honed my speaking presentations for the construction industry, but I lacked a really big component that I saw in other great slide decks: data. There wasn't great data on tech adoption or usage in construction. There were anecdotal numbers thrown around and the usual "We're number one at..." from tech providers. But there were no Gartner or thinktank reports on how the industry viewed, selected, adopted, and implemented tech.

At this point, we had several hundred construction clients and thought, "Why don't we survey them?" So we did. In 2012, we had two hundred respondents to our ten-minute survey. By 2019, our annual Construction Technology Report was publishing responses from thousands of participants and was sponsored by the largest organizations in the industry and quoted by every industry publication.

By 2016, I had done over 275 speaking gigs and had an email list of thousands of attendees from those presentations who had completed a form to download my slides from my website. If people knew me, they didn't mind listening to me. They had verified my experience and learned something new from my presentations. I realized podcasting would be a way to reach them more frequently and cover the topics, products, and people I wish I could read more about in the industries we built tech for.

So we started the first tech-focused podcast in the construction industry, *The ConTechCrew*. It helped us find other technologists, hidden throughout the industry, who wanted to geek out on the tech they were using on construction projects. Looking back, it's inspiring to note that our early guests had titles completely unrelated to tech because construction companies rarely had more than one or two dedicated IT staff members. As the industry evolved, so did our podcast guests and their roles. We now get to interview Chief Data Officers, CIOs, CTOs, IT Directors, and even Innovation Directors at construction companies. The podcast also drew out the tech providers, even competitors, who wanted to talk about what they could offer. We had become the media outlet we had been trying to reach.

Our most recent effort in becoming our own megaphone started as a way to travel the country and train our software users. Attendees also wanted me to talk to them about new and innovative construction tech they should check out. So, we built a ConTech Roadshow, and we traveled to four to six cities a year. At each event, we gathered 100–150 construction geeks to talk about the software they were using and the technology they should be considering. There were plenty of three- to five-day trade shows in the industry, so we just built a locally focused, one-day event with fifteen to twenty vendors that didn't require flights or hotels. We addressed a different audience that also happened to align with our target customers, and we were able to establish ourselves as thought leaders yet again.

All of these examples reinforce my belief that if you—the founder, the intrapreneur, the innovator—are not willing to be the Chief Evangelist for your vision, no one else will do it for you. You have to lead the messaging, and as my late friend Buck Davis used to say, "Don't let the means become the end." Always ask yourself if you're pursuing popularity or profitability. You have to make friends, help people, and see your business grow. You have to establish yourself as an expert and earn the media attention, and if your bootstrapped budget restricts that, find clever ways to *become* the media.

Innovating Insurance Tech

As 2018 drew nearer and we began to consider the sale of our flagship product, SmartBid, we knew we'd have to pursue a parallel effort to drive revenue and incentive to keep all of our staff on board and engaged if a product sale happened. We'd been building custom software for insurance companies since the early days of the company without having to do much marketing or sales. We were well known for and really good at it. And we now had this product experience that could potentially be applied to the cash-flow-heavy, tenured insurance industry. We decided it was time to really focus our mad scientists on insurance, and here's why.

We originally pursued ad agencies as clients because we thought these companies were at the forefront of tech. Their clients want digital marketing strategies and new websites—they already believe in the power of tech, so we wouldn't have to spend months pitching them on it. While this thought process wasn't wrong, it lacked foresight into the challenges of working in the advertising industry—namely, everything you produce is public; therefore, everyone has an opinion on it. Website-development projects were time consuming, very hard to scope, and even harder to stick to scope. Design and marketing decisions are heavily influenced by personal preference and taste over best practices. We learned all this the hard way.

Luckily, the one insurance client we had and the construction clients we were starting to onboard through SmartBid in the early 2000s were reinforcing the direction we needed to head next. We realized that in order to control and predict costs, we needed to work in industries that not only had cash flow but had indifferent cash flow. This is money spent regardless of the state of the economy and without needing input and approval from everyone down the chain. When I finally realized the value of working on insurance tech, I could have kicked myself for not realizing it sooner.

Insurance has been around for thousands of years. In fact, some of the very first insurance instruments were loans that you paid interest on, but the principal was forgivable if the product didn't arrive at the location (thank you, Babylon). So suppliers three thousand years ago would get loans, and if the ship didn't arrive with their goods, the principal was forgiven, but the interest was not. Well, that's an insurance contract, right? You're paying a premium that's worth the cost in case of an event. Insurance has been used for a very long time, and it's critical to society and the economy.

Bootstrapping is way more feasible when you're selling to industries that are really critical to people and the economy. You have to have insurance, and people keep paying premiums even when the economy is struggling. They may try to reduce their premiums, but they'll keep the insurance. Industries that are not discretionary, meaning consumers are likely to maintain spending in them regardless of the economic conditions, are often the most ripe for technological innovation.

The most exciting thing about insurance technology is the ROI. Insurance companies are people-heavy and data-heavy businesses, so effectively implementing new software, hardware, and processes has a broad impact. This is especially evident in the number of technology companies that start as vendors to insurance carriers and brokers and decide instead to start carrying risk and compete against them. With the data sets that tech vendors manage, they realize they don't have to be just the middleman; they can try to meet the end users' needs completely.

Pixar, when it went into the entertainment business, could have simply built software and hardware and been a vendor for traditional movie studios. Instead, it became a movie studio, automating the design and development of animated films and producing products that were much higher quality in much less time than the traditional studios. They decided not to sell to the studios; they decided to compete against them.

In so many industries, but especially personal and commercial insurance, we're seeing two kinds of tech companies: tech companies that serve as vendors to established companies in the industry and tech companies that start as vendors and then decide to jump in and compete with established companies rather than serve them. What are these companies solving? They are automating the insurance policy management process. They're automating insurance claims management. They're bringing a dramatically better user experience to quoting and buying insurance, and they are applying predictive analytics and machine learning to solve important issues that have been very difficult to solve.

There are companies that exist today that can underwrite a rental insurance policy or a homeowners insurance policy in a matter of minutes, asking you one-tenth the number of questions other companies ask because they've combined big data, public data, satellite images, and more into a data profile of your risk. They don't have to ask what your property looks like; they've got satellite images. They don't have to ask what the taxes were last year; they have access to that information. They're pulling together private and public data, and they're using it to significantly improve how individuals and organizations address risk.

Everybody on this planet has to have insurance. We have car insurance. We have home insurance or renters insurance. Either the government mandates it, your landlord does, or your family's healthcare needs do. The process of valuing and delivering insurance coverage is being chopped from days down into a matter of minutes, and it's significantly reducing the cost of risk.

There are simply fewer people and fewer hours involved in underwriting a policy and processing claims, which reduces cost. Have you ever gotten into a wreck? Have you ever had a car accident or damage to your house? Today, there are companies that allow you to submit a claim by text, work with a chatbot, answer a few questions, and take a few photos. It then runs your information through an algorithm, and in some cases, it can auto-pay the claim and issue your money instantly. We're starting to see some big shifts in the way insurance is purchased too. Think about your auto insurance; you pay premiums roughly every six months. What if you don't drive a lot, and you could just pay to insure your car for the way you drive? Progressive was one of the very first companies to start toward this trend. It was called the Progressive Snapshot. Their slogan was "Go with Progressive, and good drivers save." They added "good drivers" because their technology, an IoT device that plugs into your vehicle, turned that vehicle into a giant data-reporting machine, and your premium would increase if you drove like a bat out of hell or more miles than you initially reported. Metromile is also a company trying to turn auto insurance on its head by allowing customers to purchase insurance by the mile instead of the month—a wonderful feature for low-utilization drivers. This has been happening for some time in drone insurance (I know this from personal experience with my drone flights). You can purchase drone insurance by the hour or by the mile. You can draw a circle on a map, set a specific time and location, and buy commercial drone insurance for it. I did that because we simply don't fly drones a lot, so it's way cheaper.

Ultimately, there is a double-edged sword to all this technology that may be obvious. If you're tracking activity, bad activity will be tracked alongside the good activity. If you're a bad driver, you'll end up getting a premium increase. If you want to use your boat more, you end up paying way more than planned for insurance. If you use your drone in unauthorized areas, they're tracking it. There are always pros and cons to progress and innovation.

These types of innovation signal a much bigger move in the industry to leverage big data and machine learning to change the very fundamentals of how insurance products are priced, purchased, and utilized. But this type of innovation shouldn't only be the domain of the VC-funded startup or the extremely well-funded mainline players. Small- and medium-sized, bootstrapped companies in the industry should be experimenting with product innovation and technologies to help ensure they don't get left behind.

Insurance is an exciting industry to work in because there's so much waste that can be reduced and we, our business and our employees, can experience the benefits. The premiums can come down, and profits to the insurance companies can still go up. It's a case where everybody wins. That's why I'm excited about insurance technology.

JBKnowledge works hand in hand with many large insurance carriers, brokers, third-party administrators, and pharmacy benefit managers. We help them upgrade their technology, deliver a better user experience, streamline their internal operations, and automate processes so they're the disrupters. We are helping them disrupt their own processes before other people do. We work as advisors and developers, write the software, integrate third-party software, and automate processes. We're even using robotic process automation, where you train a software robot to perform tasks that a human would normally do. It's an intermediate step because real automation occurs after you have application programmer interfaces (APIs) that connect different products together to exchange data and automate processes. We're helping clients automate manual processes, focus their team on strategic work, and reduce costs.

We also built, almost ten years ago, some of the first mobile apps for customers to interact with their insurance administrators. Now, we're working with some of the biggest insurtech startups and insurance carriers to build the next generation of apps. I believe that in the insurance industry, we're at the beginning of what we can do to really revolutionize the way risk is calculated, priced, and covered. There are endless opportunities for mad scientists who are willing to make innovation a habit and a process. We are absolutely geeking out on being a part of it, and we bootstrapped our way into it.

CHAPTER 9

FINDING THE END OF THE RAINBOW

For two elected terms in the 2010s, I was a city council-man in my town of College Station, Texas, where I've lived for over twenty-five years. I learned a lot of things about consensus building and decisions by committees. I learned democracy is intentionally inefficient in order to slow down and vet the decisions made with taxpayer money. It's not the most efficient way to govern, but it's the right way.

At a bootstrapped company, you're not dealing with taxpayer money; it's the founders' money. At the end of the day, the founders are the only required consensus. It's important to realize the weight and responsibility of this—and what it means for your team, especially during an exit scenario.

A hard lesson I learned from selling SmartBid is that when you're a bootstrapped entrepreneur, your employees hold you, and only you, responsible for every decision. There's no saying, "The investors demanded this; it wasn't my choice!" When people ask me what the hardest thing about selling SmartBid was, they may or may not be surprised that I say, "Communicating it to our team."

While the discussion to sell SmartBid involved a ton of people, the final decision to sell SmartBid only required three approvals—myself, my dad, and Sebastian. It was our biggest accomplishment as a company and the fastest emotional rollercoaster I'd been on yet. It was the biggest sale of my life, and it involved more meetings, paperwork, and negotiations than I'd ever experienced. It felt like there would never be enough time to ask every question and have every conversation necessary to get it done. But we did. And we learned more about ourselves and our team than we could have ever predicted.

If we get another chance at an exit in the future, there are things we'd do the same and things we'd do differently. Bootstrapping is definitely not something we'd do differently. It allowed us, the founders, to maximize the equity we each walked away with from the sale and justify every dollar we'd refused to personally take home since 2001.

> **PRINCIPLE:**
> # You always get paid last.
>
> As a bootstrapped founder, your compensation should always come second to the financials of the business. Pay yourself last, even if that means not getting paid at all or until you exit.

Deciding When to Sell

In our twenty-plus years of doing business so far, our company has never taken outside investment. When we started, I said we'd never sell. I meant the company, but that also came to mean I wouldn't sell anything, a product, division, etc. Over the years, watching products and companies come and go, I learned that every product has a lifespan, even if

I never wanted to sell the company. Around 2012, when I accepted that our most successful product, SmartBid, may have a lifespan, we started to outline our criteria for selling. I spent a lot of time trying to understand what our "optimal value point" would be. This is the point at which our equity in the product would not increase in value and therefore the point at which we needed to sell. In SaaS, value is determined by several things: growth rate, customer churn, annual recurring revenue (ARR), and, sometimes, earnings before interest, taxes, depreciation, and amortization (EBITDA). In many cases with tech startups, that last one is not factored in nearly enough.

I kept analyzing those numbers and saying, "When we see an indication that these might have an inflection point, we need to start looking at selling the product." My greatest understanding of those numbers came from two main sources. One source was predictable: talking to people who'd exited SaaS products successfully. The second source was surprising to me: talking to lots of investors. After all, I didn't want an investor; I wanted a buyer.

Starting in 2011, private equity groups, VCs, and competitors called me a couple times a month about SmartBid. Whether that was due to the critical mass of customers and data we had reached, conditions in the industry, or both, it was flattering. That is until I realized they made a hundred of those calls a day. It was a sales operation. I went from flattered to frustrated. It felt like they were wasting my time, so I stopped answering.

When I accepted in 2012 that SmartBid may have a lifespan, I realized I was ignoring an incredible data source for understanding SmartBid's optimal value point: those investor phone calls. Every VC, private equity group, angel investor, or other interested investor (there's a lot of categories of investors) I could get on the phone would give me more data points if I was smart about listening and asking the right questions.

I learned to navigate those conversations to reveal little but garner a lot. I learned to end them with "Not now" and leave the door open for future conversations when we were ready to sell. I was careful about the information I gave them but took note of everything they gave me. I wanted to learn about the industry, the competition, their investment criteria, their business model, what they had to offer, and what made them different. Here were some of my favorite questions:

- What quantitative and qualitative factors are you looking for in an investment?

- Describe an attractive investment for your company and how it's different from other investors out there.

- What's your fund size and average check size?

- What information do you need from founders to have a serious conversation, like to get past the fluff and intro calls?

- Tell me about your fund's business model—how do you structure deals?

- What trends are you seeing broadly and specifically in my industry and niche?

- What do you think the next hot segment or product is going to be, and why?

When I sat back and analyzed their answers, I understood I ran a profitable company and confirmed I didn't need their capital. That wasn't our challenge. Our challenge was we would eventually near our optimal value point, the peak of our valuation.

I was learning it's hard, but not impossible, to have high growth and profitability forever—two things I think most entrepreneurs need to feel challenged and fulfilled. At some point in the life of every business or product, you really have only three outcomes:

1. You sell it for more than you have in it, and you move on to something new.

2. You shut it down because it's no longer sustainable.

3. You maintain a lukewarm outcome and skip along in mediocrity for a long time.

I think most entrepreneurs would agree that number three is the worst fate. From those early investor calls, I learned our product was valuable enough for outcome number one when the time was right.

The Myth of the Outside CEO

A very good friend of mine is a brilliant thought leader and teacher. He sold two professional service companies, ran mentoring and group coaching sessions, and wanted to build a software product for the professionals he coached that would help them manage their practices. In 2018, he built a software product using his own money until the money ran out. He had personally invested $6 million and needed to raise more. Over the next eighteen months, he raised $12 million of outside capital, then got a board and grew the revenue by around 8 percent per month.

The reality was that it was a mediocre software package wrapped around amazing content that he produced. He went through a multi-year cycle of developing this software. It was a complex business model to produce the software and the content and then help clients scale their businesses with it. There were many things they were trying to sell all at once. He did manage to get the business to $6.5 million in revenue and a paper valuation of $50 million. While he struggled through building the business, behind the scenes, his investors were plotting to remove him. My friend started to talk about bringing in an outside CEO, and some larger investors wanted to have input over who was selected.

Whenever a visionary entrepreneur tells me they think they need to bring in an outside CEO to run the company, my immediate answer, with no hesitation, is "Hell no. You don't. You need a really good right-hand person, a really good chief operating officer and integrator to help you operate. But it's your vision and your company, so you need to stay in the driver's seat. You don't need an outside CEO because then you're going to have two visionaries, and they're going to want you out of the way." In my experience, this happens at least 80 percent of the time.

My friend hired an outside CEO. His original investors colluded with the new CEO and removed my friend from his own company—where he and his wife were still majority shareholders. He still had his stock but no job, no salary, and no benefits. In addition, all of the thought leadership content he had built over twenty-plus years was no longer his either. It was property of the company. He put a lot of his money, time, and effort into this business. He also couldn't compete against the business since he had a global non-compete clause. He could still do his coaching but couldn't do it for anybody that was a prospect or a client of his original company. While this is a cautionary tale, it's not one of defeat. My friend learned the hard way that to solve a problem, you have to trust yourself to solve it, not convince yourself to step out of the way.

At his lowest point during the process of being removed, he realized he couldn't fail. If the company succeeded, he wins. If the board came to their senses and removed the CEO for another, he wins. And if he didn't breach his non-compete and did something new, he wins.

He realized he'd been given a gift. The gift of a completely blank sheet of paper—an opportunity to start again on his terms with no legacy systems, no offices, no "poor fit" clients, no investors, and no board or CEO.

Before he started his new business, he asked himself five important questions:

1. What do I want my professional life to look like?

2. What do I want my numbers to be?

3. What products/services do I want to sell and deliver?

4. What team culture do I want to create?

5. What type of client do I want to serve?

The answers became the plan for his new business. He

was able to build a new business by design—not by default. Then he got busy.

My friend bought a bunch of email databases and started sending out marketing emails. He set appointments for himself. He made hundreds of sales appointments and grew a bootstrapped coaching business from zero dollars in revenue to over $5 million in revenue in just thirteen months by sheer force of will—and simply by bootstrapping the hell out of it. He did not take outside money, and he didn't have his own capital (it was all tied up in the business he'd been removed from). The bootstrapping mentality grew strong with this one. He had to avoid all the prospects and all the clients and all the relationships he'd already built for years in the other business, but he proved there *is* a path out.

There are two big lessons in this story. One, the answer to many bootstrapping issues is sales. Entrepreneurs usually spend too much time and money on development, marketing, customer service, you name it—everything else before they figure out sales. If you can generate more revenue with the resources you have, your options open up significantly. The second, and most important, lesson here is that you don't need an outside CEO. You need a right-hand integrator who has the authority and responsibility to challenge you and the skills you struggle with. You don't need to give up your vision or your company to get that person, but you do have to humble yourself and admit where your skills are insufficient.

Watching my friend go through this as we negotiated the sale of SmartBid was pivotal for me—it reinforced every bootstrapping decision we'd made so far and made me determined to hold my ground to maximize our exit value.

Closing the Deal

I get a lot of questions about how and when we decided to sell SmartBid and what that process looked like. The decision comes differently for every founder. For me, we saw significant competitors enter and exit the market, and we saw our growth rate drop. We were still growing, but the pace of growth was slowing. From discussions with my team and peer group and all those phone calls I had with investors, I was learning the value of our equity in the product likely would not increase. Our growth rate would not sustain the spending increases needed to stay on top, and we had too much market saturation to dramatically increase the growth rate. At the time, we had over two hundred and fifty thousand subcontractors receiving bid invitations, over 1,100 paying clients, and 143 of the world's top-four-hundred construction companies using SmartBid. I didn't want to take on investors, so the best option was to sell.

At this point in 2018, I would have been rudderless without the peer group I had joined through Entrepreneurs Organization (EO). I could sing its praises and tell you to join—you should—but you can do your research on them yourself. I will say that having a peer group, no matter the organization or entity running it, has been one of the most critical factors in my success so far. I can't emphasize its value enough.

I figured out who in that peer group had gone through M&As multiple times and could share their advice. They introduced me to a knowledgeable attorney who had done over three hundred M&A transactions and was very well-versed in the process. He helped me get our package of information together, and then he helped me take that package to dozens of private equity groups, competitors, and VCs to create a prospect pool.

In any sales process, you have a funnel of your total prospects, then your marketing-qualified leads, then your sales-qualified leads, then the leads that have a proposal in their hands, and then people that have signed and accepted the sale. That's your sales funnel. The M&A process, at least from my perspective, is no different. We combined a prospective pool of buyers that had all reached out and expressed interest. We prepared our marketing literature and information. We got them all to sign nondisclosure agreements. We sent them information. They evaluated that information. Then, we moved through the steps of qualifying them and discussing tentative numbers.

That whole process took about six months from when we first met with potential buyers to when we started getting proposals in. It took another six months to close the transaction. I generally tell people to expect the exit process to take at least a year from when you start to prepare your information and put your prospect list together to when you close and get paid for your business. It can be a pretty lengthy process. You need patience and excellent advisors.

It worked out really well for me to use my deal lawyer as my deal advisor, largely because they have to do so much of the heavy lifting anyway, and I knew my market well enough to be the sales guy. I see an unfortunate trend in many entrepreneurs, bootstrapped or not. They tend to want other people to do the selling for them. While there are cases where this makes sense, I am a firm believer that the Chief

Executive Officer is also the Chief Evangelizing Officer, and the M&A process should be no different. Most importantly, *no one* will have the same drive to maximize your equity that you do as the founder. Accept that now.

I see really visionary CEOs step back, as if to say, "This is the biggest sale of my life, but I'm going to let someone else handle it." It doesn't make any sense to me. Who knows the product better than the person who first visualized it? Who knows the company better than the person who made the choice to operate in this industry? In my opinion and experience, the CEO has to be prepared to make pitches, travel, meet with potential acquirers, and really steer the process if they want to maximize the value they get upon exiting.

On that same note, as the founder of what you are pitching, you have to repeat to yourself often, "Facts over feelings." While this sale feels incredibly personal to you and your team, your potential acquirers won't look at it that way. This is a business transaction.

In all of these sales pitches, I would ask a lot of questions to understand their acquisition philosophies. I especially wanted to root out the bargain shoppers. Bargain shoppers are looking for entrepreneurs who are burned out and tapped out, who are exhausted with their business and have hit the ceiling. (By the way, I believe those entrepreneurs need a system like EOS, not an exit. They need a process for running their business that will take them out of the tapped-out zone.) Bargain shoppers target desperate entrepreneurs, so they're going to try hard to underpay. The difference between the lowest bidder for SmartBid and the highest bidder was approximately 90 percent due to bargain shoppers. If you suspect a bargain shopper, you want to get them into a position where they have to disclose their multiple range. That's the multiple of earnings that they are using to evaluate your SaaS product. Once I heard how low their multiple was, I was able to identify bargain shoppers and shut down conversations.

I learned to look for strategic acquirers. They are direct or indirect competitors or work in horizontal or vertical markets to yours. They are private equity groups who have complementary businesses they want to combine or align with yours. The best valuations I saw were presented by strategic acquirers. They had a specific plan in place for my product and a pretty thoughtful valuation due to that plan.

The key thing in the M&A process if you're an entrepreneur, or you're just starting your business, is to set your organization up properly so when you get to an M&A stage, you've built an asset that can be transferred easily, effectively, and efficiently. This will ensure it's properly valued by a strategic partner. Since I discussed selling early with our leadership team, they were able to be a part of the effort to get organized and get our pitch together, but I'll admit this took us more work than it should have simply because we didn't initially build the product with an intent to sell. Sure, we restructured in 2012 in case we did sell, but it wasn't a clean effort. Sebastian, who handled all the data, documentation, and team operations while I went out and pitched to potential acquirers, will be the first to tell you that we won't make that mistake again. We'll build every product from day one as if it may one day be sold.

Interestingly enough, the key company in SmartBid's

origin story, iSqFt, which bought BidFax and shut it down, ended up being our strategic acquirer. We sold to our biggest competitor. It was a good and fair transaction, but only because we maintained control not just over the M&A process but throughout the development of the product. Bootstrapping was *the* biggest factor in our successful exit.

You've seen the transactions and exits from venture-backed companies that are massive. They're acquired by public companies, so you can read the sales prices across news networks and social media. It feels like watching someone win the lottery. You're wondering what sports cars they're going to buy and if their parents will get new houses too. What you don't see is what the co-founders receive on their end of the transaction. In many cases, when a company that has been through multiple rounds of fundraising gets to an exit, the founders will end up owning 20 percent, 10 percent, 5 percent—sometimes even as low as 1 percent—of the business. And then there's the clever VCs who have liquidity preferences, which means they have guaranteed rates of return on their money. Even though the founder might own 5 percent of a business when they exit, they'll only get 1 or 2 percent of the proceeds because investors had a two- or three-times liquidity preference that gobbled up the returns. In comparison, a bootstrapped entrepreneur who kept their equity, stayed debt free, and built a business with a smaller exit will have much greater net proceeds.

Every time we hit a financial roadblock in the development of SmartBid, we were forced to choose between borrowing money, raising money, or reducing expenses. Ultimately, we had to ask ourselves, "Who are we trying to build generational wealth for?" Choosing to manage expenses helped us maximize our own equity and generational wealth. I'm not here to say don't take on investors; I'm here to say you should take on as few as possible. Not all venture capital is bad. Not all private equity is bad. There are great VCs and private equity firms that recognize the value of an innovator, an entrepreneur, and an active founder. They make sure not to crush founders out of their own equity. Spend the time to make sure these are the ones you're dealing with.

If you start raising money, your company lawyer is no longer your personal lawyer. You need to have your own personal legal representation to review all the documents and agreements so they can protect your rights over your equity. They can ensure when the exit occurs, there's not going to be clauses from the investment contract that get triggered and end up halving (or even quartering) the amount of money you receive on the exit.

It's a very complex game, and the people who play this game are intelligent. They have taken a lot of measures to protect their investments and maximize their returns. Remember, at the end of the day, their responsibility as investors is to the people who gave them the money to invest. That is who they are ultimately responsible to, not you.

In my case, from 2001 to 2018, we were able to maintain the freedom and control we wanted over the business, including the SmartBid product. We were able to bootstrap and maintain our equity. We were able to maintain control over the direction and vision of the product. We were able to generate cash and grow the business. We were able to make it profitable. We used our services to make profit along the way, and we used our products to build equity value. Most importantly, when we sold, we kept almost all our staff and immediately started working on our next product.

You May Celebrate Alone

The day we sold SmartBid and the funds officially hit my account was an anti-climactic day. I was traveling to our Seattle ConTech Roadshow, and I was sitting at my gate in the Dallas airport, waiting to board. Suddenly, I had more money than I'd ever imagined in my bank account. I was by myself, and I remember thinking, *How am I supposed to feel about this?* Don't get me wrong—I was excited, but I was also exhausted. We'd spent nearly a year in this process. The final months were a gauntlet of emotions, staff meetings, reassuring clients, and saying goodbye to some of the best people I'd ever worked with. On top of that, we had a plan for moving forward, but I was still apprehensive. *What if we can't do it again? This team is trusting I made the right decision. What if I let them down?*

Startup teams are gritty, scrappy, and willing to put in extra sweat for experience. They bond quickly and get used to fast pivots and hypergrowth. They don't give up easily, and sometimes, to them, exiting *looks* like giving up. In 2018, we had three divisions in the company—Products, Services, and Consulting. The teams were heavily integrated and in some cases—like marketing, design, R&D, and customer service—shared. We had nearly two hundred employees, and most had worked on SmartBid at some point if they had been at the company longer than two years. I knew what selling this product would mean to our team. Since we hadn't been through a transaction like it before, it was going to take a ton of communication to avoid scaring or disappointing everyone.

Sebastian and I met with the leadership team first for long days of discussions and debates on how and if we should sell. There were two executives in particular who almost exclusively worked on SmartBid. These conversations were not easy, and they were not vague. But we trusted each other enough to have them.

From there, we explored our options for nearly twelve months before making a final decision. When the decision was made, our leadership team was tasked with communicating, in person, the decision to each of their teams through group and one-on-one conversations, as necessary. After those conversations were completed, I addressed the entire company to reiterate what their executives had told them. It was a messy, difficult, emotional process. Some employees felt betrayed, confused, and scared. We went into the process with eyes wide open, and we went into every conversation with three critical points:

1. We will keep as many employees as possible.

2. You can ask any questions you need to, and we will provide the answers we can.

3. Yes, we already have a plan for what's next.

The process taught us that you can create organizational clarity through overcommunication, but you have to help your team get comfortable with incomplete information. At the end of the day, you have to build trust with your team so they believe you are making the best decisions you can with the information you have. That trust has to be built years before monumental changes and exits occur.

At the end of the day, though, as a bootstrapped founder, you're going to make the bulk of the money from the sale, and that doesn't sit right with everybody. They don't remember you paid everyone more than yourself for years or that you had years with no paycheck so you could keep staff on payroll. When recessions or pandemics hit, we adjusted our founders' pay so we never had to adjust anyone else's. We delayed employee raises a couple times, but we never lowered salaries.

When employees hear you're making a sale, it sounds like a lot of pain for them and a lot of money for you. Unfortunately, your response cannot be to list out the things I just did. Those things don't matter to them. You chose to take on that role in the company. So you have to figure out what makes your team feel appreciated and valued with a transaction like this happening. That's where you focus your energy. You don't focus any energy on justifying the money you're about to make personally.

In an exit scenario, you should take care of your employees. You can do that in many different ways. You can offer holiday bonuses or equity in what you build next, or you can take the proceeds and invest in all the things your employees have been asking for. (You should know what these are if you're listening and walking around often.) An additional step I took was helping negotiate the salaries of the handful of our employees who our acquirers made offers to—they wanted them to come with the product, but they weren't obligated to. I negotiated the salaries, benefits, and titles I knew those staff deserved.

Above all, you want to help people celebrate the

accomplishment of an exit and feel appreciated in the win. If you're not sure how to do that, ask some of them. Brainstorm with the leadership team. The worst thing you can do is righteously say, "I earned this money, and they'll be fine."

Another aspect of helping your team transition is helping your clients transition as well. We spent an insane amount of time prepping client communications, calling our biggest clients, and coordinating messages with our acquirers. We wanted everyone on the same page when talking about the sale, and we wanted our team empowered with a strong message to handle upset clients. What I learned from that process is despite some upset, our clients were overall impressed with how much we communicated with them. There had been many M&As in the industry that year, and they usually found out by seeing a new "Powered by" logo in their software. One of our most successful communications was a recorded discussion between me and the CEO of ConstructConnect, the company that bought SmartBid, about why the sale was happening and what it meant for our users, team, and industry. I was a podcast host after all, so we did an interview.

Ultimately, we determined the best way to take care of our team through the acquisition was to be decisive and have a plan for what came next. It's easy to make a bunch of money, not "need" it as badly anymore, and shy away from risk. We were determined not to shift into capital-preservation mode and out of innovation mode. So leading up to the sale, we had a plan for our next software product. We came up with a code name, communicated the plan to the team, and gave them enough info to start digging in and getting excited about it. I wanted to motivate and inspire everyone, including myself, toward something new. We only turned over fifteen people in the acquisition of SmartBid, who either left voluntarily or went with the sale of the product to work for the new company. I knew if I didn't figure out the target to set ahead of myself and everyone else, we'd be aimless.

Finally, there was an even more personal team I had to prepare for this big change. I knew that I owed my family and my health a reprieve. I wasn't sure how to achieve this while still motivating everyone forward, but I figured it out as I went. My kids deserved to share this win. The best way I knew how to do that was to give them time that was long overdue. We planned family vacations. I promised and delivered weekends off. We stocked up on what we needed for new hobbies, especially ones we could do all together, like flying and camping. But Monday through Friday, I was still there for my team, working toward the next milestone of success.

The Freedom to Focus

Many product-management lessons came from the sale of SmartBid. The most important was this: build your product as if you'll sell it one day. Keep clear delineation and documentation of budgets, teams, and efforts. Give a dedicated team the freedom to focus on the product so in their spare time, they're thinking about ways to make it more valuable.

We started developing SmartBid in 2006. By 2009, we built a dedicated software-development team, customer service team, and sales team. By 2015, we had finally hired dedicated marketing and design resources. By dedicated, I mean each employee on those teams was tasked with prioritizing the SmartBid product and minimizing time spent on other divisions or products in the company. Many of the first hires on those teams stayed with us until the sale of SmartBid, and that tenure and consistency were paramount to the success of the product. We learned, a little slower than we should have, the value of dedicating and focusing teams on one product at a time. While SmartBid was slowly receiving that focus, it was at the expense of another product we were developing: SmartCompliance.

In 2009, we developed SmartCompliance, a certificate-of-insurance–management software, after realizing that risk management teams, both at insurance brokerage firms and big corporations, had to track, issue, and/or collect certificates of insurance from all their vendors and partners. This usually involved emails, PDFs, and spreadsheets. We knew we could build something better, and we did. We also built a modified version of the software as an add-on to SmartBid. We knew the SmartCompliance product was great, but we never gave it the focus needed to help our target market understand that.

Since selling SmartBid and refocusing those sales, marketing, design, development, and customer service teams on SmartCompliance and our newest product, Terra, we've seen exponential growth. We quadrupled our revenue from SmartCompliance in four years. While this could be attributed to the experience these teams now have, I can safely say these products could not have achieved the same success as SmartBid when we controlled it because they weren't given the same prioritization. Our product teams knew the size and importance of SmartBid, and even if they aimed to spend X hours a week on another product, it was hard to justify switching their focus to a smaller product when the time came.

In building our newest product, Terra, I've also seen a noticeable difference in how our team thinks about and approaches their work. After seeing the success of SmartBid, they understand the end zone a little better. They understand the length of time it can take to build a sustainable (and sellable) product. They understand the growth trajectory required, and they understand the risk involved and why we do it.

As our software-development services division grew over the years, we saw a need among the major insurance carriers around the world to benchmark and measure incoming insurance claims against industry standards to determine payouts. We decided to build a software, called Terra, that could do just that—but when I took the idea to some of our service clients, they didn't seem interested, mainly because they couldn't visualize it. We asked if they would give us feedback as we built something they could click through. So we spent six months just building out a clickable prototype with our analysts, developers, and UX designers. Rather than slowing us down, this process allowed us to get critical feedback before developing any code. We spent time and money on learning instead of launching a failed MVP. During the process, we were also selling our clients. They loved getting to shape the product, and instead of waiting until we had a product to start a six- to twelve-month sales process, we were selling as we were building. We had signed clients by the time any code went live because they were so excited to finally get their hands on it.

With the proceeds from the SmartBid sale in the bank,

we've had the funds to focus on selling SmartCompliance and the patience to build Terra with an entirely different product-development mentality.

While our first bootstrapped exit awarded me the financial freedom I'd wanted for so long, I would say the biggest freedom it gave my team was the freedom to focus. This doesn't mean our future products and every effort associated with them will be perfect; it just means we're a little wiser about how we go about things, and I like to think our teams will be healthier for it.

CHAPTER 10

KNOW YOUR LIMITS

What comes after the biggest sale of your life?

James Clear says, "Doing it right is hard. Doing it over is harder." The sale of SmartBid was my biggest success as a bootstrapped entrepreneur, but that doesn't mean it'll be easy to do it again. Success takes discipline, and I'd argue discipline is hardest once you've tasted success. It's easy to drink your own Kool-Aid and say, "I know what I'm doing now," but all paths to success won't look the same. The only guaranteed constant in my past and future successes is me, so I'm the only one who can set my terms for doing it all again.

Bootstrapped entrepreneurs have to be willing to iterate and follow their intuition toward each success. As a bootstrapper, you don't have the capital to wait until you've explored all options to the fullest. You don't have anything called, or remotely resembling, a runway. Your runway is a month or two long, and that's it. Maybe longer if mortgaging your home, laying people off, or selling assets is an option. But most of us are ambitious, principled innovators who won't even consider those options. So instead, we have to get really good at pivoting on a dime and making decisions with incomplete information.

This is so much easier said than done, and paralysis by analysis is real, especially when your personal and professional worth is tied up in your business. Since the sale of SmartBid, learning the concept of personal minimums from my flight training and applying that to my future business endeavors has significantly helped me reduce my own analysis by paralysis and make quicker decisions.

In pilot lingo, a personal minimum is the minimum weather conditions you're willing to fly in. These vary based on the pilot, their experience, and their plane. Each time I decide whether to fly or not, I have a minimum set of requirements that aids my decision. For example, I will not fly with less than forty-five minutes worth of fuel in the tank, even though thirty minutes is the legal requirement, and I will not fly in thunderstorms.

Having personal minimums is important, but it's even more important to communicate those minimums to others who can hold you accountable and support the decisions you make within those minimums. I learned this the hard way when we had to delay a family vacation by days because thunderstorms would not let up. My daughters were really frustrated that I wouldn't fly until I explained to them why not flying in thunderstorms was an important personal minimum for my and their safety.

As our company pivots to new products, I've learned about the power of documenting and communicating our personal minimums as a leadership team. Having minimums gets everyone to step two of every decision immediately so we can continue to innovate and build efficiently.

Here are some of my personal minimums at work:

- I will not travel more than two to three days per week, and I won't travel three weeks in a row. I learned the hard way how that affects the team at the office and the team at home.

- I will not miss leadership meetings on Mondays unless I'm on vacation. That is the team that needs me more than any other, and I won't miss it for clients or any other meetings.

- My children's school holidays are on my calendar and assumed to be days that I also take off unless there is an emergency; I'll sometimes work from home, but my team knows I won't be in the office those days.

- When I need a nap, I take one, even if it's only fifteen minutes.

Team minimums also help us evaluate efforts and pivot without our egos getting involved. For example, on R&D

projects, we may set a minimum requirement of X customers by X date to continue beta testing a product, and if we don't reach those requirements, we shut down the effort and move on quickly. Pivoting doesn't always mean shutting something down, though. Sometimes, you're just too early; sometimes, you haven't found the right market, and sometimes, it just needs to go on ice until the budget or time frees up enough to test it some more.

By establishing personal minimums and team minimums, then communicating them, your organization has parameters to operate and experiment in without needing your daily guidance or approval. They can get to step two of decision-making quickly. You and your team are able to make rational decisions based on parameters you've already set, not based on emotion. Ultimately, you're able to achieve more as a team because you've identified parameters that lead to success.

The Power of Checklists

My grandfather, my mother's father, was a pilot in the United States Navy. He flew seaplanes in the South Pacific, looking for submarines during World War II, and then flew reconnaissance missions over the Bering Straits in Alaska. Later, he was responsible for aerial intelligence that came off of the Bay of Pigs in Cuba.

After my parents met and married, my dad got his private pilot's license and had my mom get her private pilot's license so if something happened to him while flying, she could fly the plane instead. My first flight was probably when I was three months old. My first international flight was before I

Establish and communicate your personal minimums.

After a big success or failure, you start to see the path traveled more clearly. You can especially see where communicating your vision, expectations, and deal breakers would have helped everyone navigate the path better. Document and start sharing those lessons in every effort moving forward.

was one. I've done thousands of hours of trips all over North America, and I fell in love with flying at an early age.

I began my own flight training when I was nineteen. I was in the middle of starting my college internships and about to launch my business, but I didn't get my license. I completed all the training and my solo cross-country flight and just never took the final test. Once the business got started, I didn't have the time or money. It wasn't until I was thirty-eight that I got my pilot's license. Not getting it sooner is one of my biggest personal regrets because flying has made me a better human and entrepreneur.

When I finally received my license, like most things I do in life, I went all in. I bought my first airplane and got my instrument rating. (An instrument rating allows you to fly in clouds and fog—your pilot's license is really just your license to learn.) There are over six hundred thousand pilots in the U.S., and only half have an instrument rating.

Flying is one of the few things I do that settles my multitasking brain because it is so all-encompassing that there's really not much else you can do but fly if you're doing it right. You have to pay attention to everything—the weather, the instruments, the navigation, the airplane, your destination. I had forgotten how much I love learning something really hard and engrossing. My "thing" for so long had been "being an entrepreneur," and I had forgotten I had time to be more "things." If I could be a "pilot" at age thirty-eight, what could I do at fifty? And sixty? And seventy?

I talk a lot about entrepreneurism, and especially bootstrapping, granting you the freedom to control your destiny and make your own choices. I don't think there are many freedoms bigger than the ability to decide you want to go somewhere, get in your own plane, and go there. It also helps that there is an enormous amount of technology involved in aviation, and it gave me a whole new set of gadgets, functionalities, and user interfaces to experience and inspire me.

Flying has given me new perspectives on focus and technology, but the physical perspective it provides has also had a huge impact on me. The beautiful thing about being in the cockpit is you have the best view in the airplane. You can see everything, and your brain seems to stretch out to fill that view. Every pilot becomes a philosopher. It's hard not to when you see the world at that height and breadth. It changes and shapes your thinking, whether you realize it right away or not. I'm envious of astronauts and can't even fathom how their worldviews change, literally and figuratively, through space travel.

As someone who has rarely lacked confidence or words, flying has also been incredibly humbling for me. As soon as you feel like a great pilot, the weather, the plane, or air traffic control chimes in with a reality check.

I've learned the most sensitive time while flying an airplane is during takeoff. After you've been flying and when you're about to land, if your engine goes out, you can coast and then glide onto the runway. There's no coasting during takeoff.

So, in order to take off and land safely, we have checklists. I have physical copies of them in my plane and acronyms to help me remember them quickly. Before becoming a pilot, and before Malcolm Gladwell introduced me to the concept of flashbulb memories, I would have told you that checklists are only necessary *some* of the time.

Flashbulb memories are memories about specific, significant moments in time—like September 11, 2001—usually because they were shocking or surprising. The belief is that our memories from those events are vivid and detailed because the event had such a profound impact on us, but the reality, discovered by researchers, is that our flashbulb memories vary over time.

Research shows that our memories, even in these big moments, are wrong more than half the time. Researchers had people write down their memories immediately after 9/11—where they were and what they remember happening. A year later, they had them do the same thing, and the story would be slightly off. As time passed, the stories continued to skew from the original. A few years later, people would even start denying their own handwriting from their first accounts of the day. Their brains were reprogramming that flashbulb memory.

What did this teach me? If my memory is only half correct when it comes to *big* events, how good can it be in remembering mundane flight checklists? Not very good. Our memories are unreliable, so when I'm flying an extremely complex machine in an extremely complex environment, checklists are everything.

Flying has taught me that documentation and checklists are not an effort to slow you down this time; they are an effort to make you faster next time. In bootstrapping, the speeds of decisions and innovation are however long it takes to send an email or make a call. You're operating with little bureaucracy and little democracy, and this is great. What's not so great is how the lack of documentation affects future decisions and innovation.

Imagine if you made a checklist every time you figured out the most efficient way to test a new feature, and imagine that checklist is accessible to every new developer you onboard. We've built checklists for hiring, onboarding, development, quality control, customer support, design, marketing campaigns, events, client retention, and employee reviews. Name a team in our company, and it has at least one documented checklist, likely five to ten. Every single meeting we run across the company has a checklist to keep it focused and on time.

If you're still not convinced, I'll add that the more documentation and checklists you can show to a partner, investor, or acquirer, the clearer they can see the efficiency and value of your company or product. Especially if they are hoping to merge your organization with one of theirs, if they can visualize how processes intersect, they are much more likely to see value.

Never Stop Studying

Another monumental lesson I learned from flying was the importance of training and continual learning. If you're a good pilot, you read all the time. There are many podcasts out there for aviation that share safety reports and stories on airplane crashes so you can learn from what went wrong.

Several stories are stamped in my mind and run through it every time I fly. A pilot flying from Houston to a small Texas town called Kerrville forgot to double check his fuel levels and started with an erroneous calculation. He ran out of gas suddenly mid-flight, and no one on board survived. Another pilot forgot to take their parking brake off, and during take-off, the plane veered through a fence, killing him and his family. A pilot in Atlanta reached up to adjust a setting without looking and pulled the wrong lever, turning off his entire avionics panel. I check the seal on my airplane doors multiple times before takeoff now because I read of a pilot whose doors weren't sealed and water seeped in and froze at altitude, which pushed the door open and depressurized the cabin. Listening to these stories, I've realized I have to constantly study to stay safe as a pilot. I've also realized I don't give studying and learning enough energy outside of flying. As a leader, I have an obligation to continue learning, and the most tangible and fulfilling way to hold myself accountable is to set and track attainable milestones. There have been very few professional feelings that were better than passing my flying check rides. They were all very difficult for me at the time but rewarding to finish and pass. In business, I don't think we give ourselves enough of those achievable short-term milestones. When's the last time you picked a new certification or skill or took a course and completed a test?

This simple mindset change, sparked by learning to fly, unlocked a new area of my brain that I forgot existed. I now set annual personal goals every year—a third of them have to do with flying, a third are personal hobbies, and a third are work related. I have nearly five years' worth of milestones mapped out to hit.

As an entrepreneur and "the boss," it's easy to think you're the smartest person in the room. You are most impactful, though, when you're learning alongside your team. Flying has reminded me of the discipline of studying and learning. It's reminded me of the importance of leading myself, not just a team, toward milestones. I've since received seven ratings and flown over 1,200 hours.

The Value of Time

I spoke at nearly four hundred events before we sold Smart-Bid. Each event represented one to two nights in a hotel, twelve hours of driving, parking at and sitting in airports, and a day of adjusting to the rhythms of my family and the office after I returned home. I didn't add up all that time until I started flying and understood the value of driving to the closest airfield, getting in my plane, and taking off immediately.

Through personal experience with thousands of clients, I know that entrepreneurs all too often undervalue time—their own time and especially their team's time. They don't think through the monetary value of time and how much it's costing them to use it. Time feels like the only "free" resource in a bootstrapped startup, but we all know it isn't free. In fact, it's your most valuable, non-renewable resource because you only get to spend it once, then it's gone. The bad news is that no one can tell you how much an hour of your time is worth and where you should spend it—that depends entirely on your company's current stage and future goals. I wish I could say I've developed a simple formula.

I do know that every time I fly my plane instead of booking a commercial flight, I consider the cost of my airplane depreciating over time, the cost of fuel, the cost of my airplane hangar, and the cost of parking. When compared to a commercial plane ticket, the economics don't make sense; I should probably just book commercial. But when I compare these numbers to the time I'll save traveling to and from airports, waiting to board, and connecting and picking up baggage and multiply that by the number of employees I'm able to fly with me, the math starts to make sense. The math makes sense when you figure in the cost of your time *and* your team's time. Never forget that part of the equation in every business decision.

If you aren't already tracking your or your team's time, I can't stress the importance of the practice enough. It has nothing to do with Big Brothering how they're spending their time and everything to do with understanding where they focus their day. We didn't get good at this until just before we sold SmartBid. You can set the example by tracking and reporting your time in the next leadership meeting. Share where you spent the most time, where you realized you wasted time, and where you should have spent time. Get your team comfortable talking about how they spend their time and asking for help in prioritizing it. Time is a bootstrapped company's MOST valuable resource, and when you actually work on quantifying it, you get really serious about how you're spending it.

Supplying Bootstraps

In 2011, I started my career in local politics on the Planning and Zoning Commission for College Station, Texas. From 2012 to 2018, I served as an elected city councilman. Though these positions were unpaid, they allowed me to support the city that helped me build my business. Participating in the decision-making process that affects our communities and businesses was fulfilling, enlightening, and definitely frustrating at times.

In May 2020, I applied for a governor's appointment to various boards and commissions in the state of Texas. I wanted to serve an entity that impacted the industries I work in, like technology or insurance. They called and said, "We don't have a position for you on anything you applied for, but we're hoping you'll consider serving on the Texas Southern University Board of Regents."

As I stood holding the phone, listening to their pitch, my mind transported me back to 1995. I remembered the day Southern University, an HBCU, offered my high school a free high-speed internet connection. If the day I got my first computer at age twelve was the day I fell in love with technology, the day I first connected to that high-speed internet was the day technology and I said our vows. My science-fair win, my first tech consulting business, the computer science teacher who introduced my co-founder Sebastian into my life—all of these things and more happened to me thanks to Southern University's generosity to a bunch of nerds down the street. There was no way I was turning down this opportunity to serve an HBCU in my own state, so I accepted.

"Exceptional financial need" is the criteria for receiving a Federal Pell Grant. Eighty percent of the students at Texas Southern University use Pell Grants to attend the school. This means it's not just books and rent that are expensive for them; basic needs like food and clothes are as well. I've never known that kind of hardship. Working with these students and knowing that despite their financial circumstances, they chose to go through weeks of paperwork and years of study to create the future others couldn't give them is inspiring to say the least.

It's a well-known statistic that lifetime earnings for an individual are tied to their highest level of education. The problem is the biggest universities in each state, especially Texas, mainly accept the top 10 percent of applicants. The next tier of universities may accept the top 25 percent. That means over 65 percent of high school graduates have to find other options for higher education in community colleges, small universities, or trade schools.

The magic of Texas Southern University is that it serves an underrepresented population who want to be educated but can't afford it. It provides a place where they feel supported by educators who know where they come from and peers who came from there too. I thought Texas A&M had the strongest sense of community and belonging I'd ever experienced, but Texas Southern is on another level.

Working with these students and educators has emphasized for me that so many in our country are born without bootstraps and without someone to teach them how to use them. It's pretty hard to start a business when you're focused on basic needs like food and shelter while trying to complete your education. These students are not looking for millions of dollars to fund their startups; they're looking for a small loan to buy a laptop. They could be doing both, but they may never have been taught that. A small business administration (SBA) loan could change their lives. They likely didn't grow up with mentors who ran successful businesses. It's hard to find mentors when you've never known that kind of relationship and aren't sure how to ask.

You'd think my first focus as a Regent at Texas Southern would be in the business school, but I actually jumped into the aviation program. There is a vast, nationwide shortage of pilots right now, and there's always been a shortage of pilots from underrepresented groups. Underrepresented groups don't see people like themselves in the aviation industry, so why would they pursue a career in it? I'm hoping to help change that. Our program allows students to earn their pilot ratings and a four-year degree at the same time. We provide an affordable path to becoming a pilot and turning it into a career. I'm hoping that path also inspires them toward more freedom through entrepreneurship someday.

For so many of our students, entrepreneurship is a few hundred to a few thousand dollars and one mentor relationship away. My position at Texas Southern has inspired me to reach outside of my own circles to provide mentorships and funding. If I only produce more entrepreneurs that grew up like me and look like me, I'm not truly paying it forward. If I'm paying it forward, I'm earning the bootstraps I had all along.

EPILOGUE

No matter what you're leading—a company, a product, or a project—I hope my ten principles and the stories that helped me arrive at them remind you there is a way to self-fund your ideas, maintain control of your vision, and build a healthy, sustainable business. Any business of any size can be its own VC and avoid having to trade ownership for cash. If you have already raised money or you're an investor yourself, bootstrapping principles can help you get the most value out of your equity. You can start applying these principles at any time. Some of these principles I learned as a kid, some I practiced as a young adult, and some I'm still perfecting.

The ultimate reward of my twenty-plus-year journey in bootstrapping has not just been financial but more so in how I and my team live our lives. So many business leaders say their goal in retirement isn't to *not* work; it's to work *when* they want, *where* they want, with *whom* they want, and *on what* they want. Our leadership team gets the unique privilege every day of charting our own course, making our own truly independent decisions, picking whom we work with, and deciding what projects we work on. That level of control over our destiny has led to drastically higher satisfaction with our professional and personal lives and, I believe, allows us to focus on doing the right things for our customers and teammates every day. As I finish this book in 2022, the economy is faltering, inflation is skyrocketing, and companies are laying off workers in an effort to control costs. The stock market is struggling, and the seemingly endless funds of VCs and private equity firms are starting to pull back and force their investments to generate a profit. Organizations that understand bootstrapping principles are going to be best suited for this era of business, where raw unit economics cannot be upside down and where growth alone is not enough—companies must be financially sustainable.

As you embark on any bootstrapping effort, the desire for an exit will be ever-present. The desire for that ideal retirement, wealth, security, and a vacation will haunt you. No matter how many detailed checklists, lessons from your dad, or amazing co-founders you have, there will be days, weeks, and months when the struggle won't feel worth it. No matter how poetically I write, I can't get you through those days. You have to know your own "why" for those days, but I thought I'd share mine.

I bootstrapped so that I could keep my family out of debt and because I was willing to sacrifice short-term income for long-term wealth. I bootstrapped because I wanted to direct technology I believed in without investors overriding my vision. I bootstrapped so I could make the decisions I felt were best for my team. I bootstrapped so I could make money doing things I was good at and have the freedom to experiment with things I'm passionate about. I bootstrapped because my father, Sebastian, our team at JBKnowledge, and I believe in building sustainable businesses that spend less than they make, achieve high growth, and have healthy, growth-oriented cultures and teams and most certainly not cultures that are willing to win at any cost.

After twenty years of bootstrapping, we're proud of what we've done, we still love going to work, and we're excited about what we're building next. I want that for all entrepreneurs and intrapreneurs. What do you want for your company, yourself, and your family? Regardless of your answer, I'd argue bootstrapping can help you achieve it.

Go be your own VC, enjoy the ride, and geek out!

MY 10 BOOTSTRAPPING PRINCIPLES

1.
Cash is king.

Nothing beats cash on hand, especially in an economic disruption. To build a sustainable business, seek opportunities to generate recurring cash with low overhead.

2.
Get out, and stay out, of debt.

Use debt as little as possible and pay it off as fast as possible. When revenue declines, debt has no sympathy and can't be cut as quickly as expenses.

3.
Build what you have to so you can build what you want to.

It will take time to build your dream business if you want to maintain control of it. Figure out what you have to build to earn revenue and cover expenses now so that you can generate profit to build your vision later.

4.
The number one rule of business is to survive.

Above all else, you must stay in business long enough for good things to happen. This means making tough decisions that drive the long-term viability of the business, not short-term or unsustainable results.

5.
Choose your partners wisely.

Anyone who has an equity stake in your business should be chosen slowly and wisely. Alignment in your values and vision is more important than any dollar amount or business plan.

6.
Get out and sell.

If you want to build your vision, you have to be the Chief Spokesperson. No one else is going to have the drive to build your dream for you.

7.
Be willing to rewrite your rules but not your values.

Values must be known by all, followed by all, and used in every corner of the business; they should not be subject to ready change. Company rules, conversely, must be flexible enough to adapt to shifting cultures, changing operations, and innovation.

8.
Make innovation a habit and a process.

People, processes, and tools—you need all three to create a culture of innovation, but the most often neglected is process. Every other function of a sustainable business operates on systems and best practices learned from generations of professionals—innovation should be no different.

9.
You always get paid last.

As a bootstrapped founder, your compensation should always come second to the financials of the business. Pay yourself last, even if that means not getting paid at all or until you exit.

10.
Establish and communicate your personal minimums.

After a big success or failure, you start to see the path traveled more clearly. You can especially see where communicating your vision, expectations, and deal breakers would have helped everyone navigate the path better. Document and start sharing those lessons in every effort moving forward.

ABOUT THE AUTHOR

James M. Benham is the co-founder and CEO of JBKnowledge, a multinational technology and consulting company he's bootstrapped for over twenty years. From his college dorm room to over 270 employees in the USA, Argentina, and South Africa, he's led JBKnowledge to build industry-leading software for the world's largest insurance companies. James has served as an elected city councilman, an adjunct professor at Texas A&M University, and a Regent on the governing board of Texas Southern University. He is a sought-after keynote speaker, having presented at over four hundred industry conferences worldwide, and hosts a popular bi-weekly podcast. James lives with his family in College Station, Texas.

jamesbenham.com

🐦 : @JamesMBenham
ⓕ : @JamesMBenham01
🅾 : @JamesMBenham
ⓘⓝ : @JBenham

Made in the USA
Columbia, SC
01 October 2024

43299146R00126